# HASHI

# HASHI

## THE BRIDGES PUZZLE

**ALASTAIR CHISHOLM**

WALKER & COMPANY ✦ NEW YORK

Published by Walker Publishing Company, Inc., New York
Distributed to the trade by Holtzbrinck Publishers

All papers used by Walker & Company are natural, recyclable products made from wood
grown in well-managed forests. The manufacturing processes conform to the
environmental regulations of the country of origin.

Library of Congress Cataloging-in-Publication Data has been applied for.

ISBN-10: 0-8027-1560-5
ISBN-13: 978-0-8027-1560-9

Visit Walker & Company's Web site at www.walkerbooks.com

First U.S. edition 2006

1 3 5 7 9 10 8 6 4 2

Book design by John Candell
Printed in the United States of America by Quebecor World Fairfield

# ——— ARE YOU READY TO CROSS THE BRIDGE? ———

Welcome to Hashi, another devilishly addictive puzzle from Japan! In this book are 202 brand new brainteasers, but beware—Hashi is easy to pick up but almost impossible to put down . . .

## THE BRIDGES

Hashi's full name is Hashiwokakero. It means "Let's build bridges!" and that's exactly what you have to do. Here's an example:

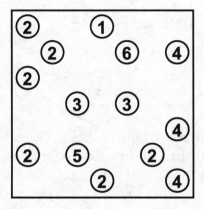

Every circle is an island; your challenge is to place bridges between them so that all the islands are connected. The number in each circle represents the number of bridges (lines) that must touch that island, thus, an island of size ② must have two bridges touching it, while an island of size ⑥ must have six bridges.

The rules for placing the bridges are:

- They must be vertical or horizontal (no diagonals or wiggly lines)
- They can't cross other bridges
- You can't have more than two bridges between any two islands
- Each island must be able to reach every other island

Every Hashi board has one and only one solution—can you find it?

## TIPS FOR SOLVING HASHI PUZZLES

The trick with Hashi puzzles is to look for large islands with only a few neighbors. If the island is large enough, and the neighbors few enough, you can often narrow down to only one possible move.

Have a look at the sample puzzle again:

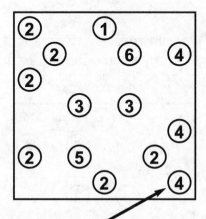

Look at this island at the bottom-right: The island is size ④ and only has two horizontal and vertical neighbors—one north and one west. Because the size is ④ it must have four bridges, and you can't have more than two bridges between any two islands, so the only possible solution is to have two bridges pointing north and two pointing west, like this:

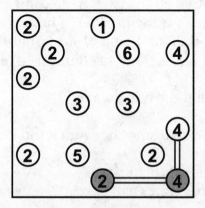

(Do you see how we've shaded in the ④ and the ②? It's a good idea to do that whenever you've "solved" an island—when you've found all the bridges—so that you can stop worrying about it. When all the islands are shaded in, the board is solved!)

Now that we've shaded in the ② we know it can't be used for any of the other islands. Have a look at the ① at the top. It only needs one bridge, but now it only has one island it can reach—the ② to the west. So we can fill in another bridge, like this:

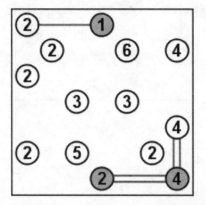

Here's another trick. The island at the west of center is size ③, so it must have three bridges. But it only has two neighbors (south and east). Remember, you can only have up to two bridges between two islands, so we know that there must be one bridge going to one of the islands and two bridges going to the other. So we can draw in one bridge south and one bridge east, and worry about the other bridge later, like this:

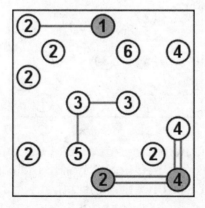

The island isn't solved yet—we still have to work out where the third bridge goes—but we've made some progress.

With just these techniques you can solve this whole board.
Here's the solution:

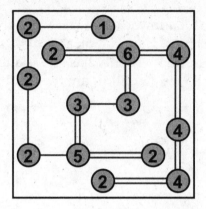

## ISOLATIONS

The techniques so far will be enough for the easier levels, but
you'll need something smarter after that. The key to advanced
Hashi solving is to remember that to solve the puzzle all the
islands *must* be connected—and you can use this to help you
make progress. Here's an example:

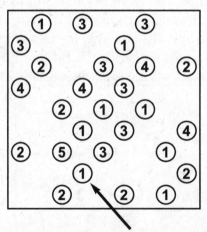

Look at the ① near the bottom-middle of the puzzle. It needs
one bridge and has two neighbors, north and east. But what
would happen if it went north? If it did, it would be connecting
to another ①, using up its only bridge, and the two islands
would be *isolated*, and thus not connected to the rest. So, the
bridge can't be pointing north; it must point east, instead.

There's another example with the ② on the bottom row, on the left. It has two neighbors, north and east. But its neighbor east is also a ② so if all the bridges went east, both islands would be isolated. So we know that at least one bridge must be pointing north.

*BACKING UP*

Like all logic puzzles, Hashi has its fair share of "erk" moments—when you realize you've zigged when you should have zagged and now something has gone terribly wrong on the board! Perhaps it's a complete disaster, or perhaps just a nagging feeling that things aren't right. What can you do about it?

First, use a pencil! When you start playing Hashi you might take several wrong turns. Just back up by rubbing out the lines. How far do you need to back up? It's hard to say, but keep erasing until you feel confident. Go back to the start if you have to!

Second, take your time. It's easy to get a run where the bridges are just falling over themselves as you write them down, but stop a moment for a sanity check before drawing in each line. Better to not make the mistake in the first place than to try unpicking a mess (and also you get to feel morally superior when you solve the puzzle without any corrections). And if you get stuck, walk away for a bit and come back with fresh eyes. There is always a logical next step to make.

## THE HASHI CHALLENGE

Now you know what to do, there are over two hundred more puzzles for you to get your teeth into. We've graded them from Delicious to Vicious—how far can you get?

Good Luck!
Alastair

LEVEL **1** | DELICIOUS

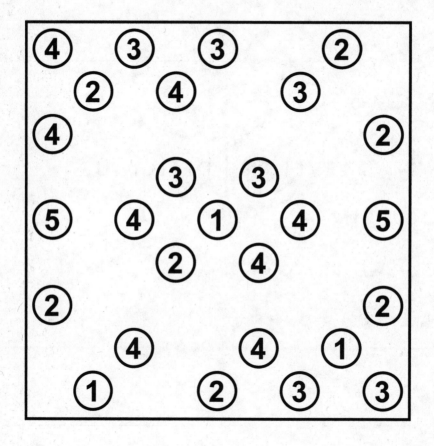

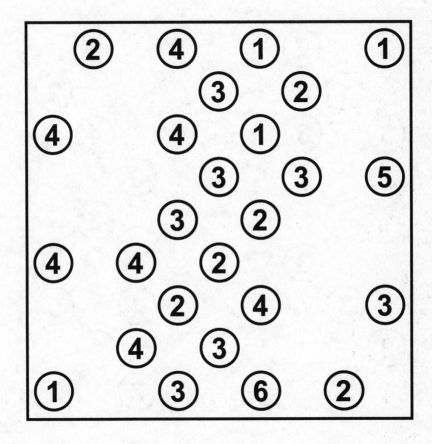

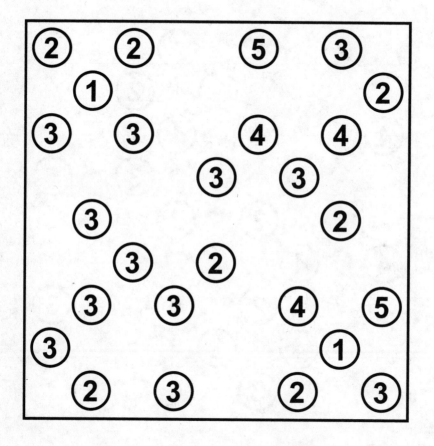

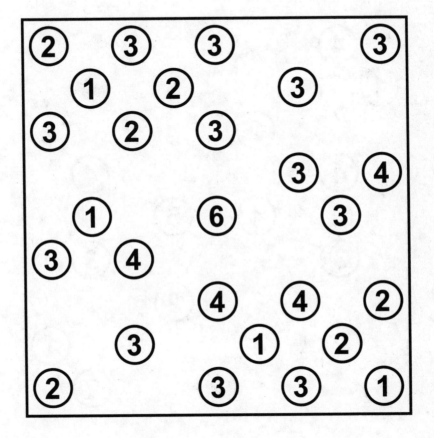

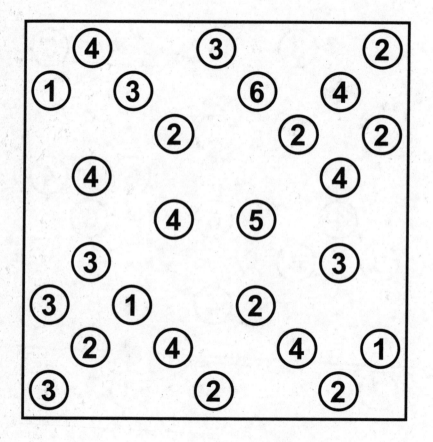

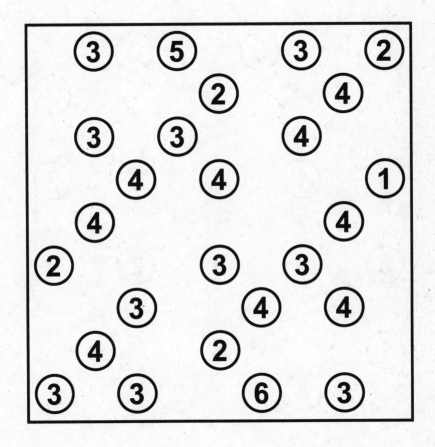

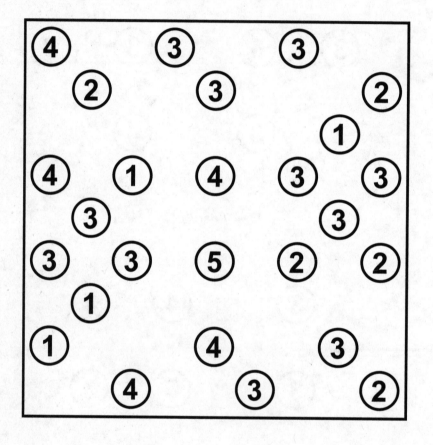

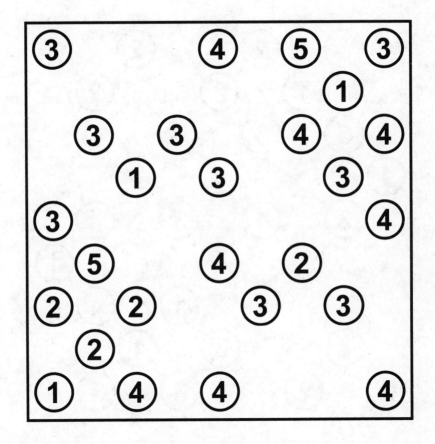

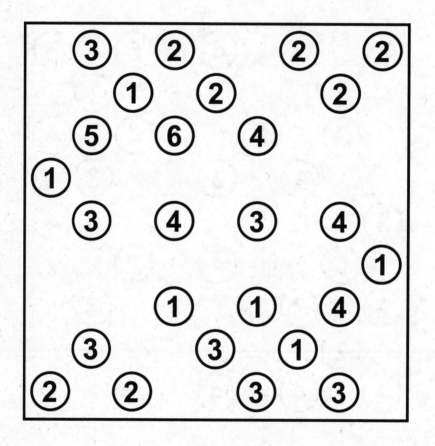

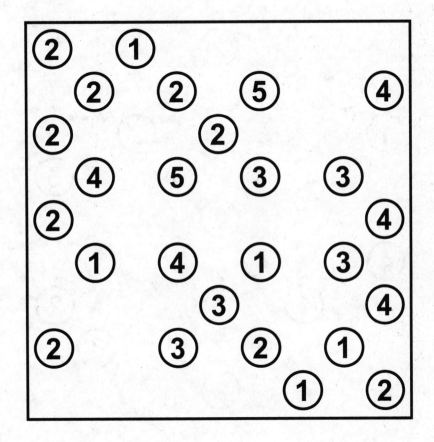

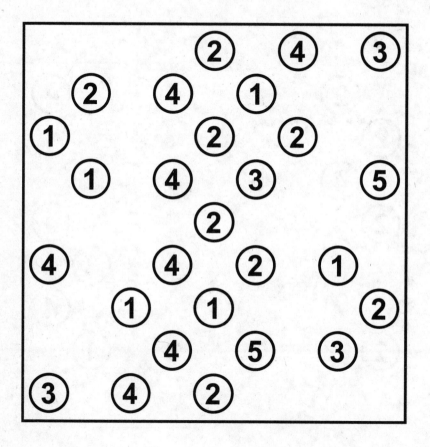

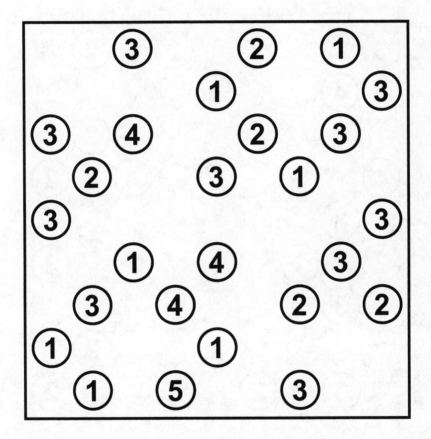

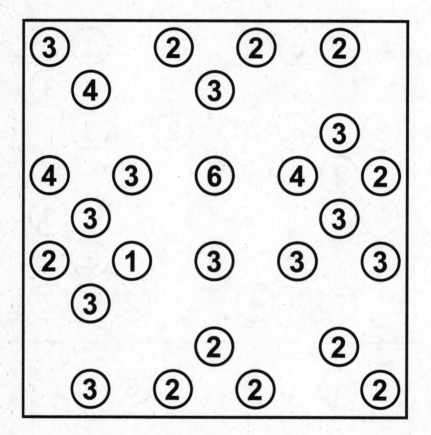

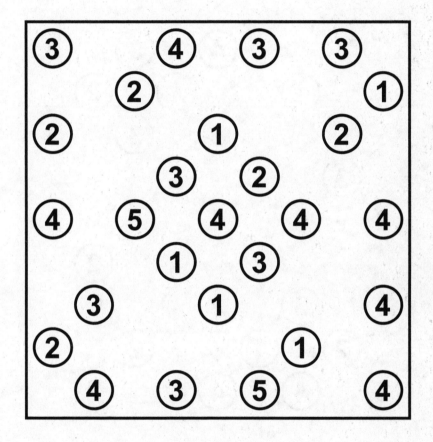

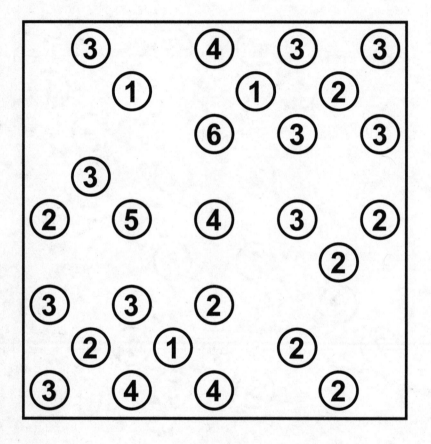

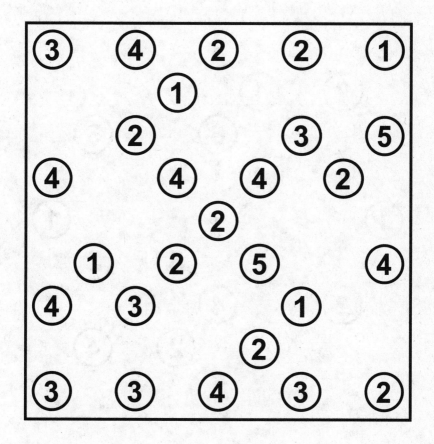

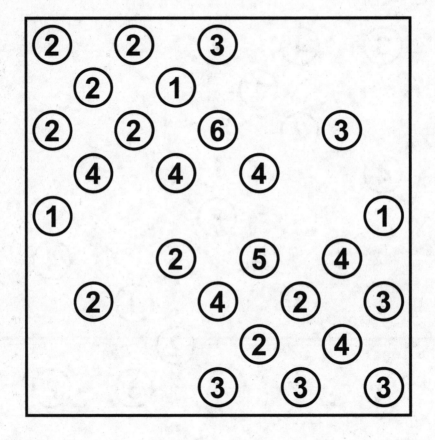

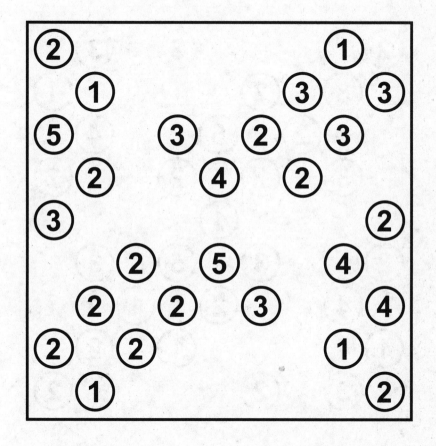

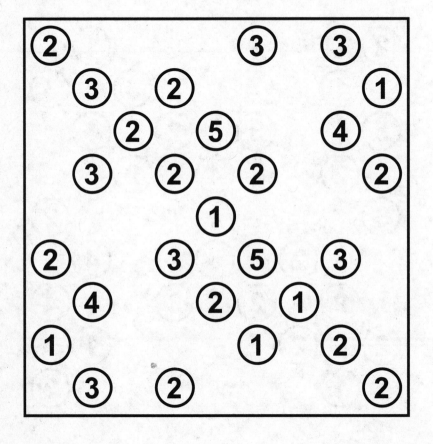

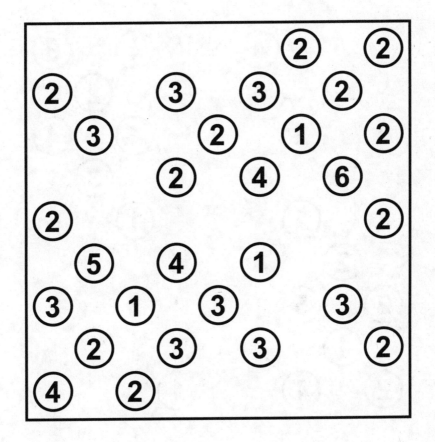

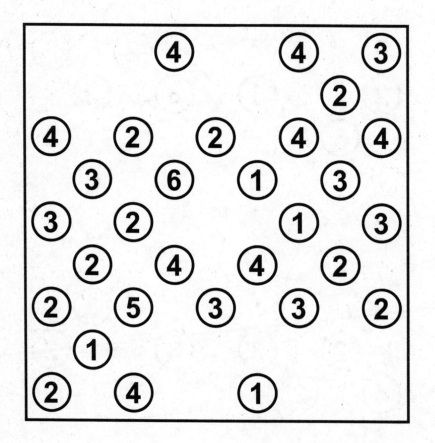

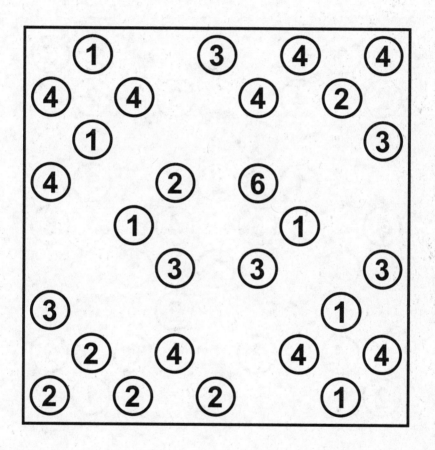

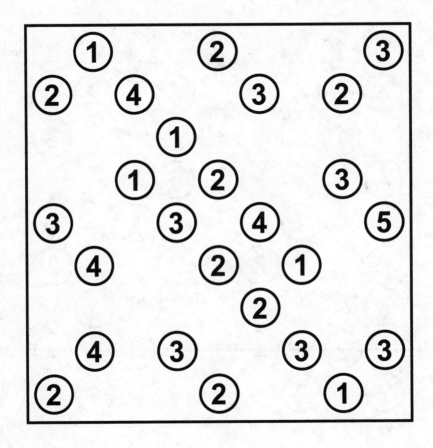

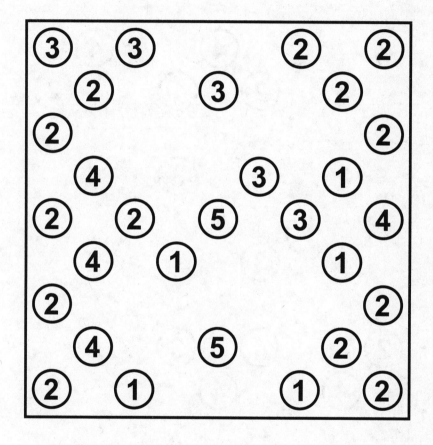

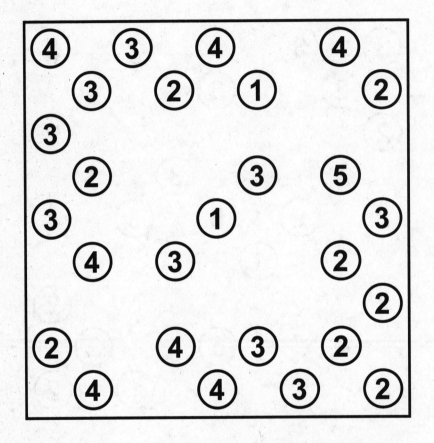

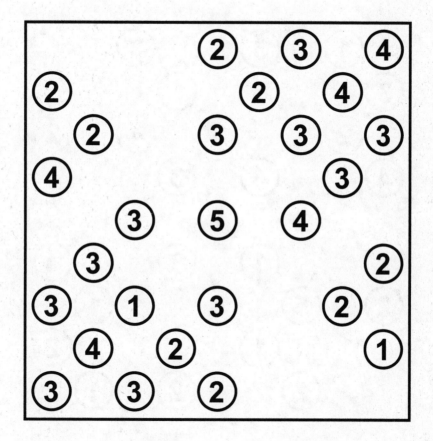

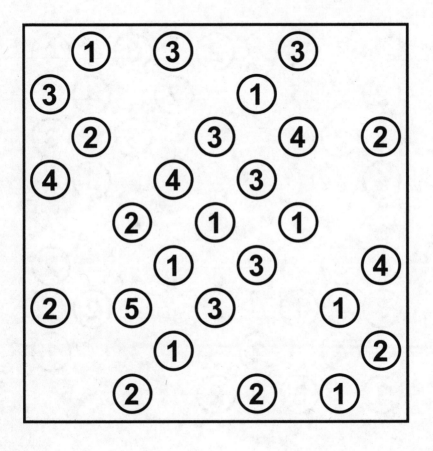

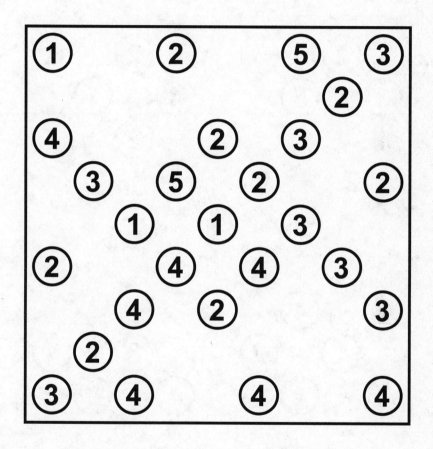

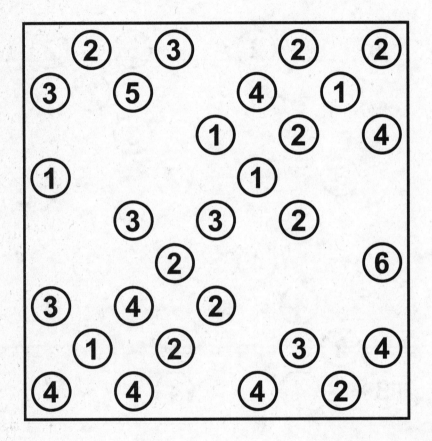

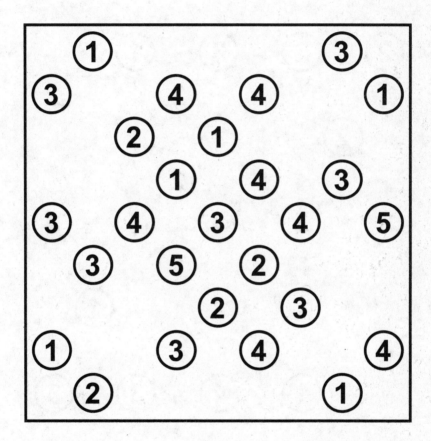

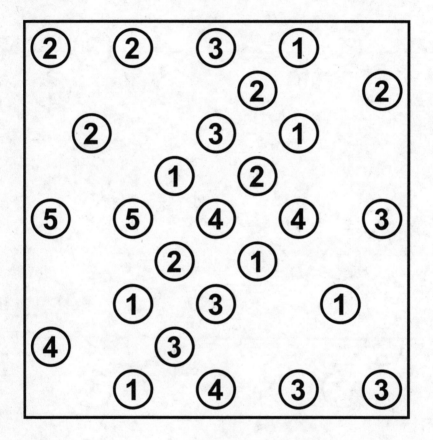

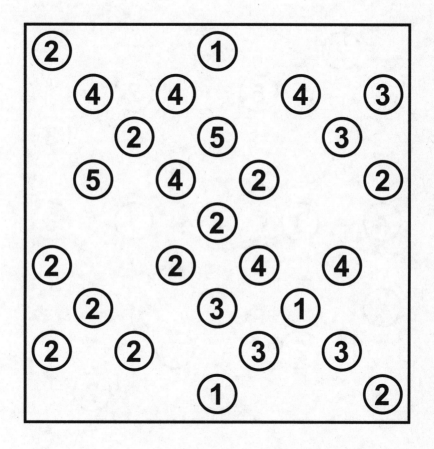

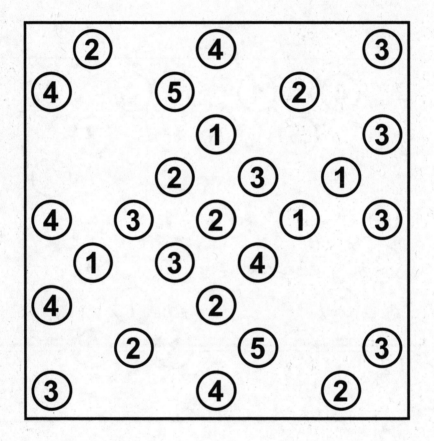

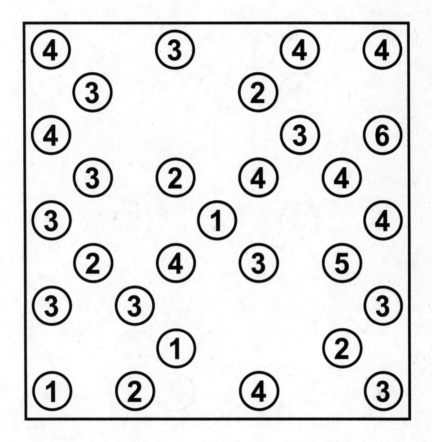

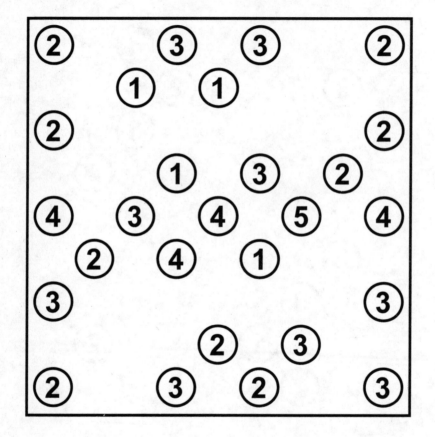

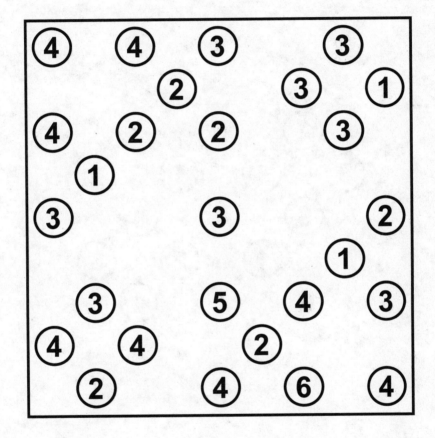

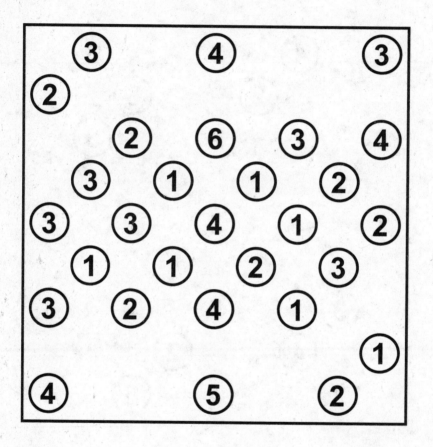

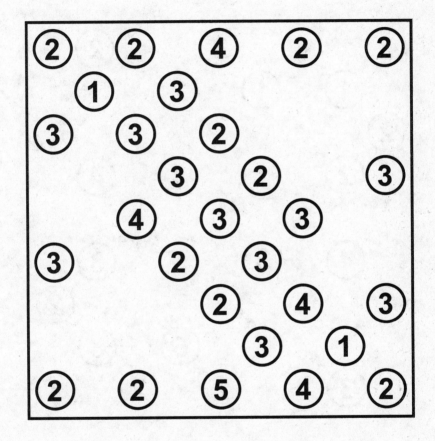

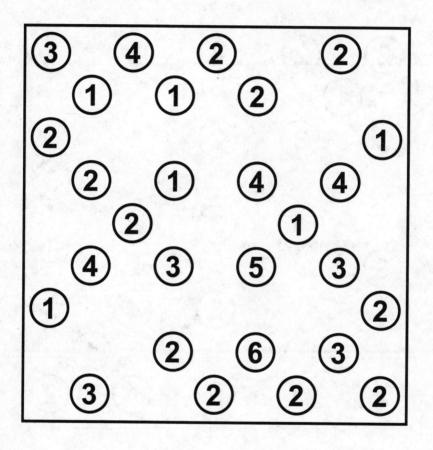

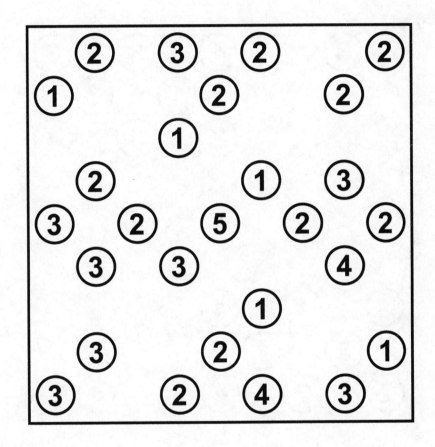

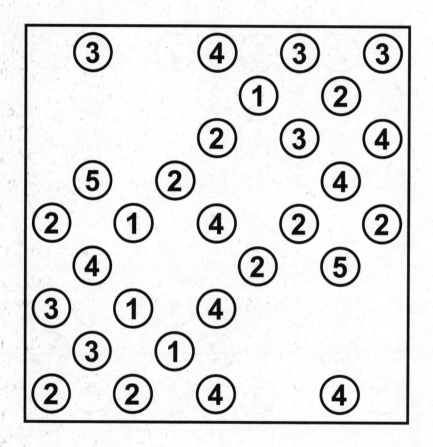

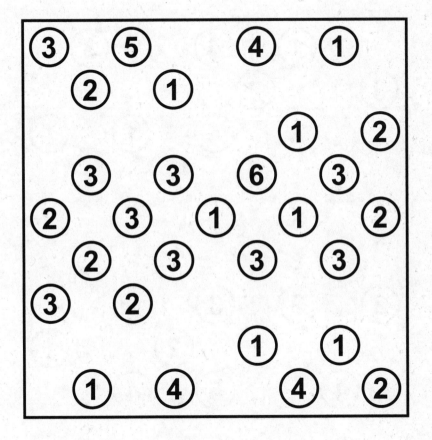

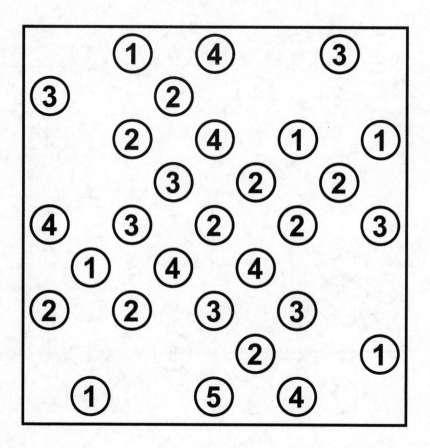

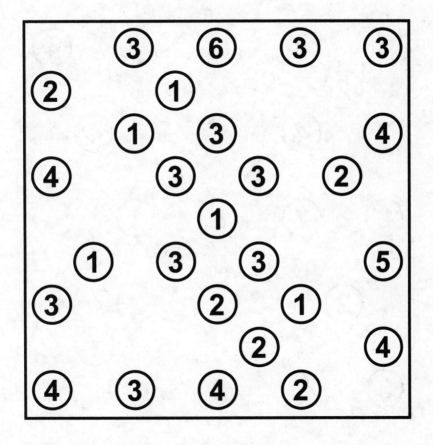

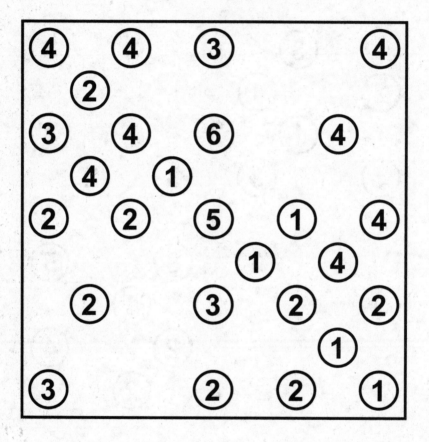

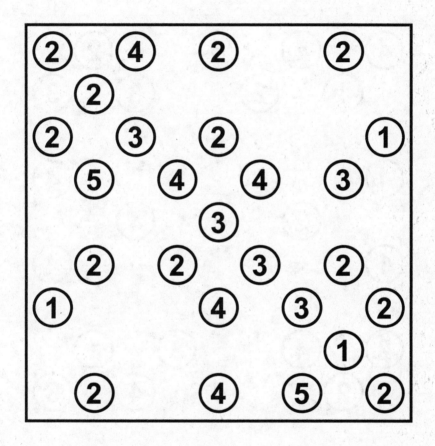

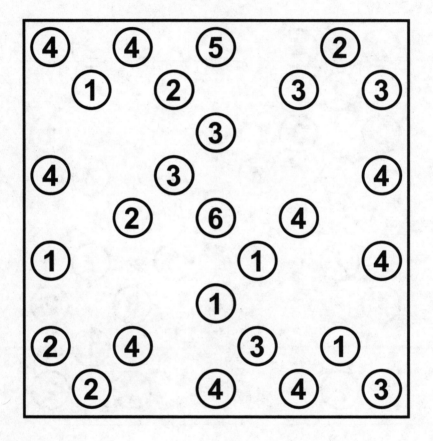

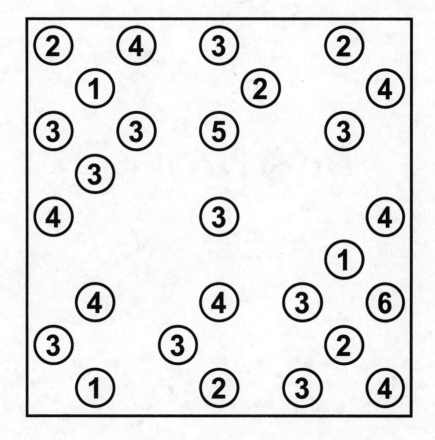

LEVEL 2 | PERNICIOUS

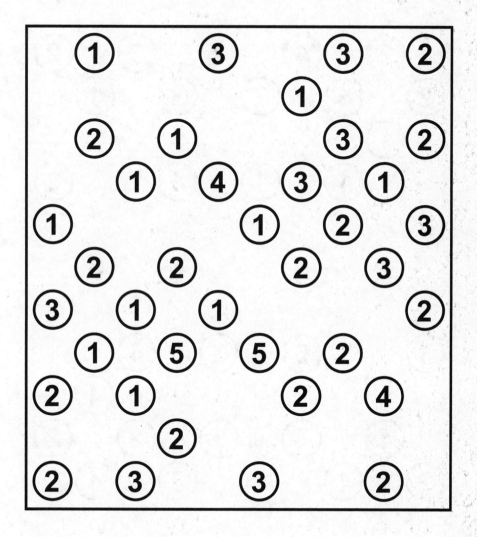

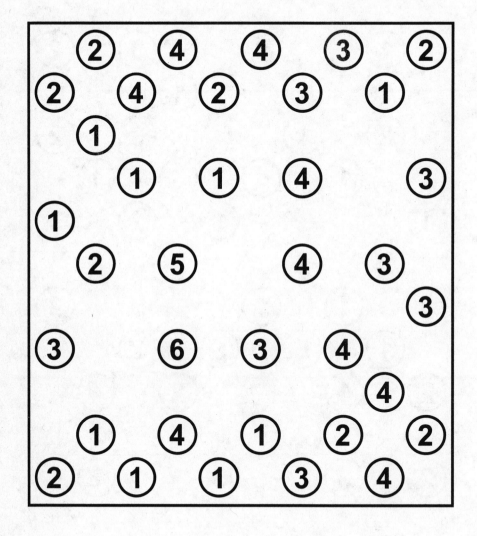

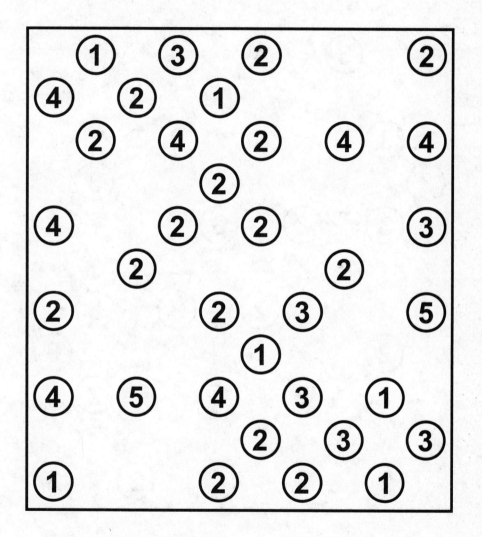

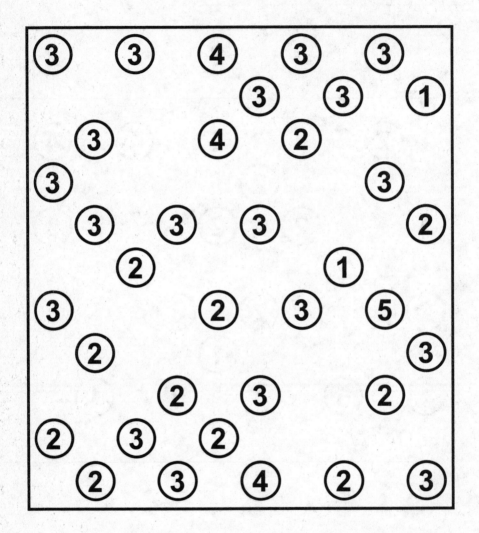

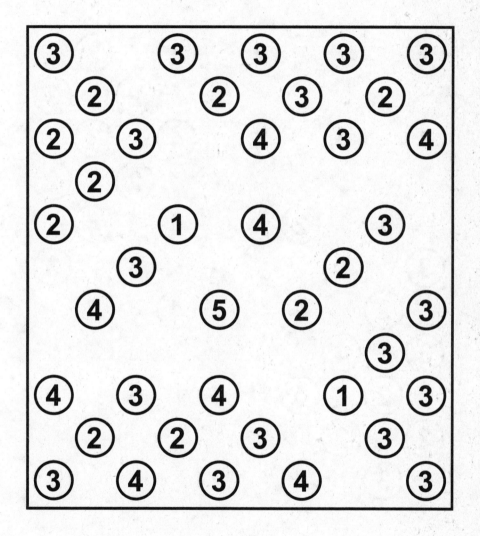

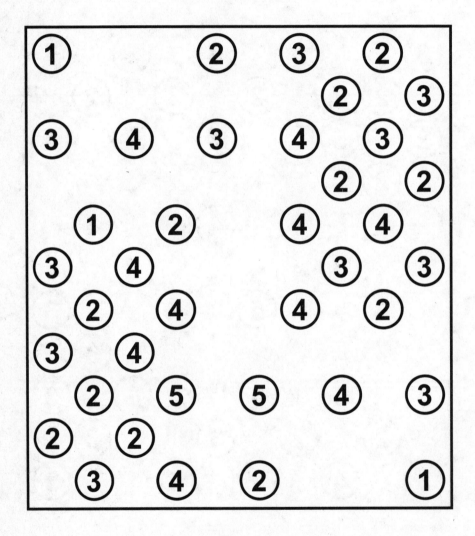

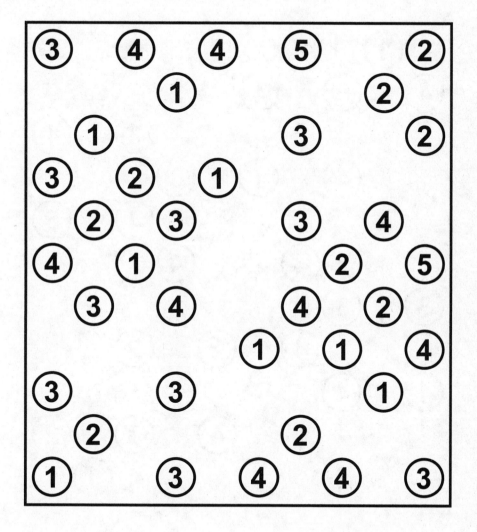

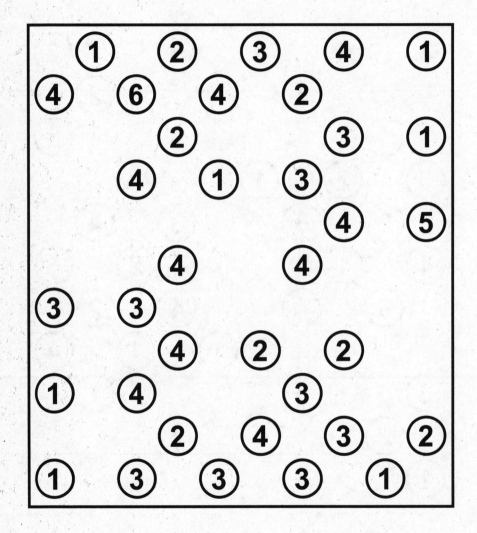

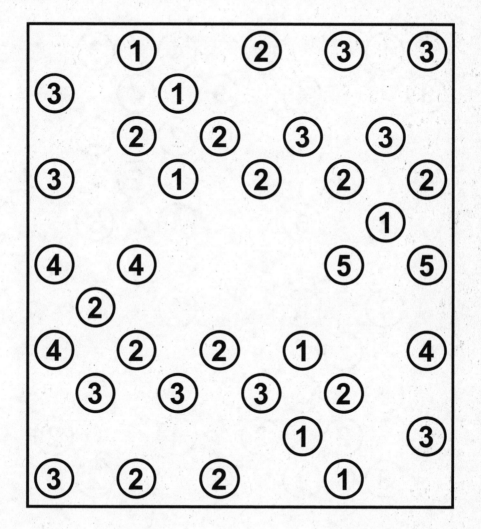

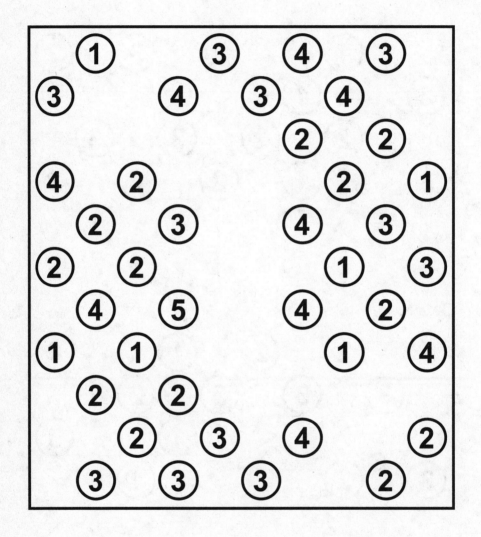

① ② ② ③ ③
　① ② ② ②
③ ③ ③ ② ②
　② ③ 　③ ④
② 　 　 　
　② 　 ③ 　
　 　 　 ③
④ ⑥ 　④ ①
　② ② ① ③ ⑤
② ② ① ③
　③ ④ ③ ③ ④

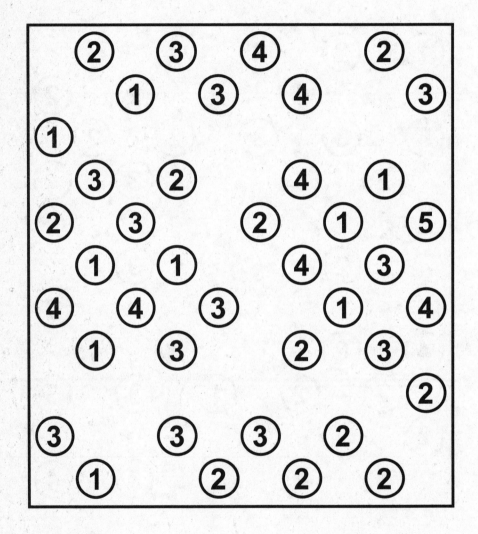

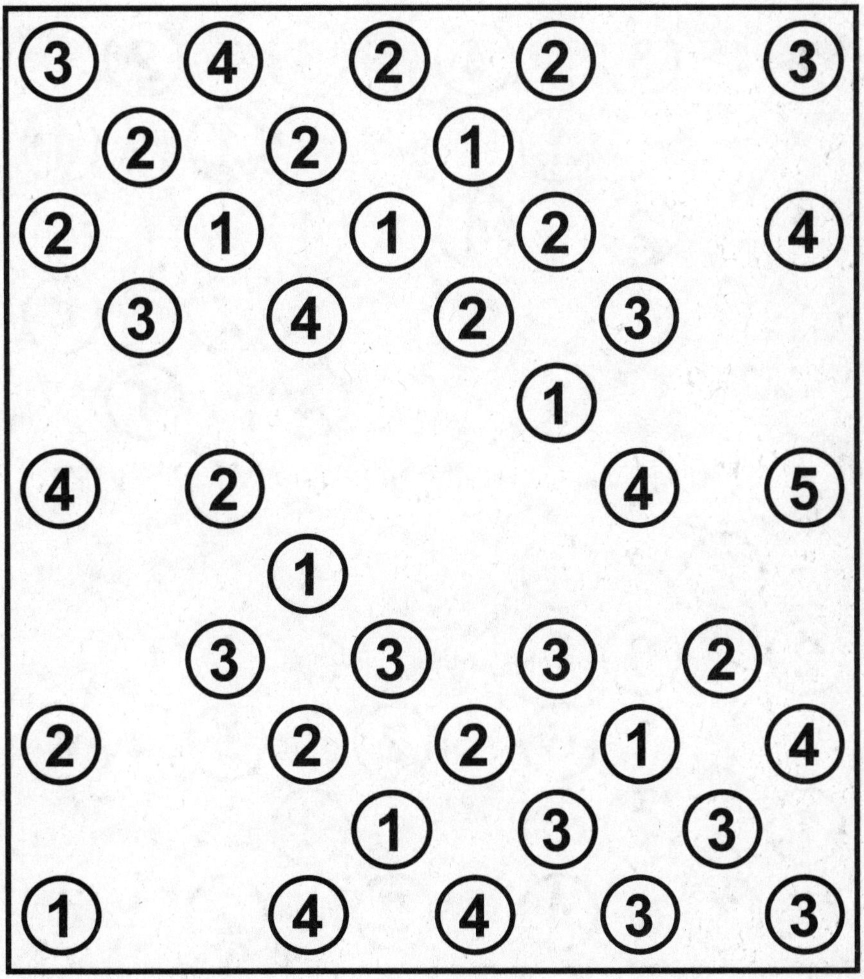

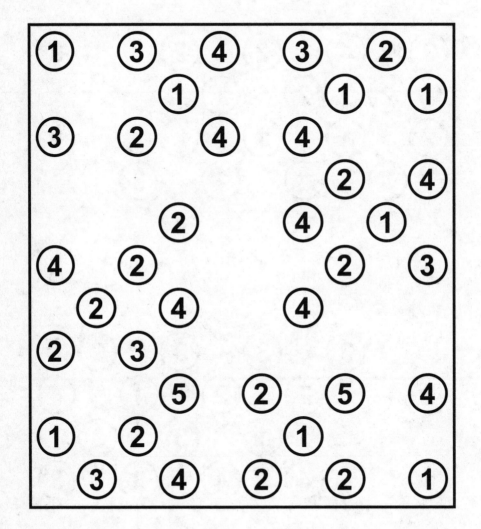

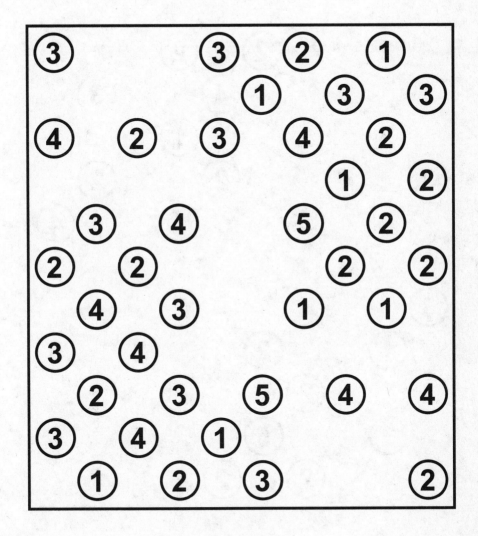

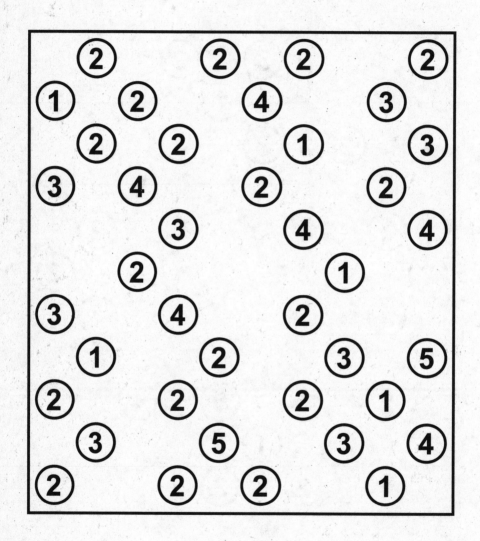

②  ②  ②      ①    ③

   ①  ②  ②      ①

③  ①  ②

   ①  ③  ③    ②    ④

         ②

④      ②      ③      ④

         ①

③  ①  ⑤  ⑥  ①

            ①    ①    ③

   ②      ③  ③  ①

②  ②      ④    ④    ③

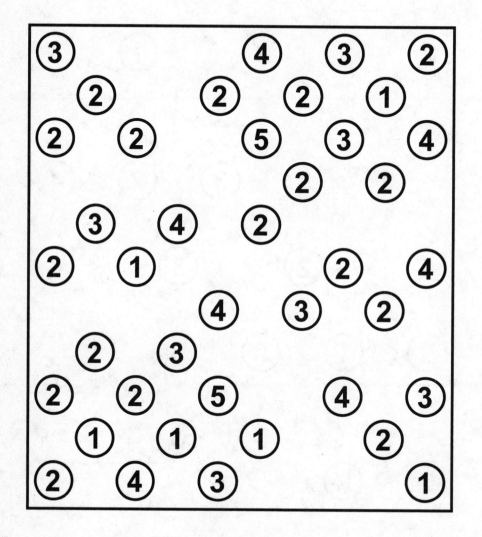

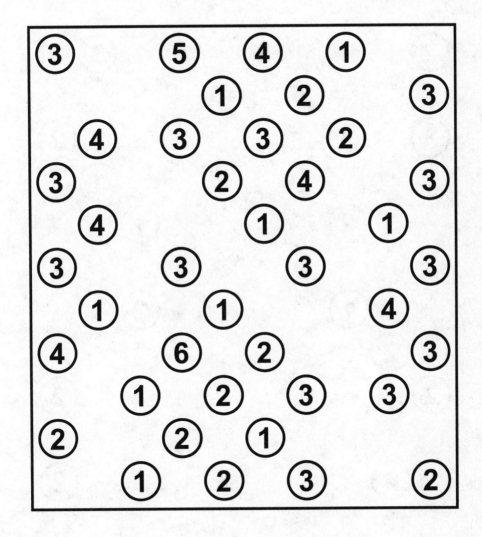

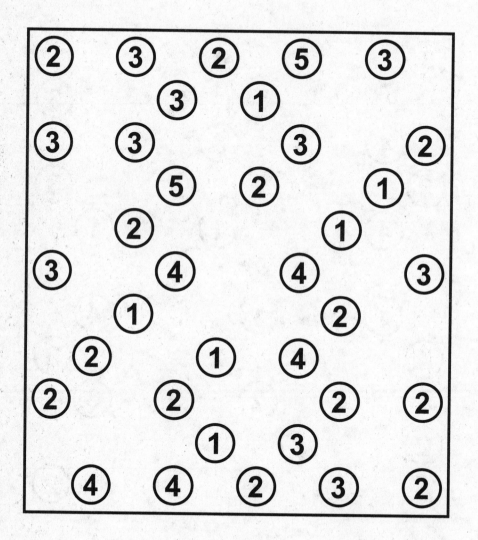

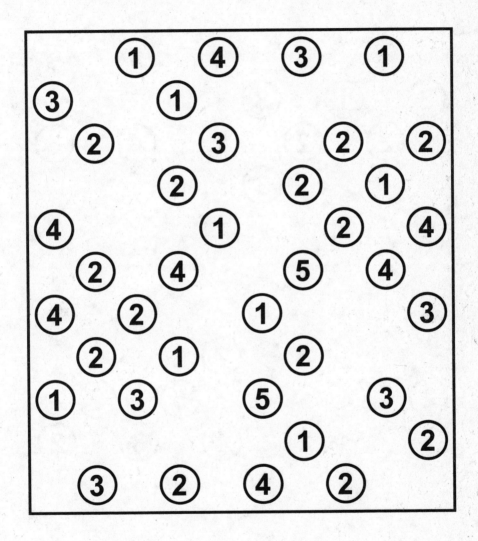

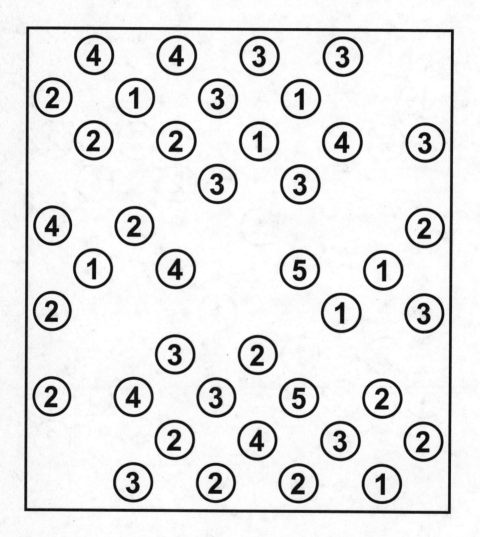

①　②　　②　　②
　①　③　　②
②　②
　①　③　②　③　③
②　①
　②　③　　④　②
　　　　　①　④
④　④　②　⑤　③
　　　　　①　④
　②　　①　①
④　　②　　②　③

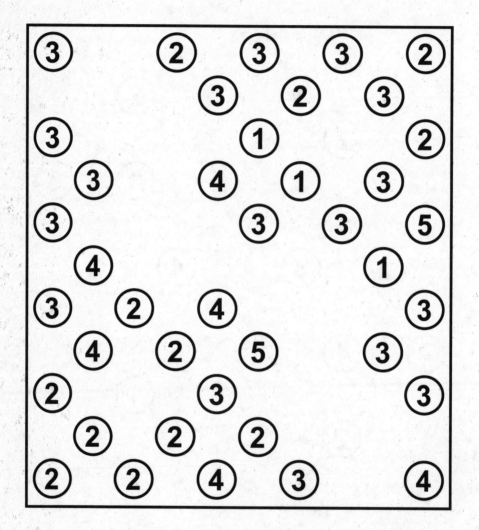

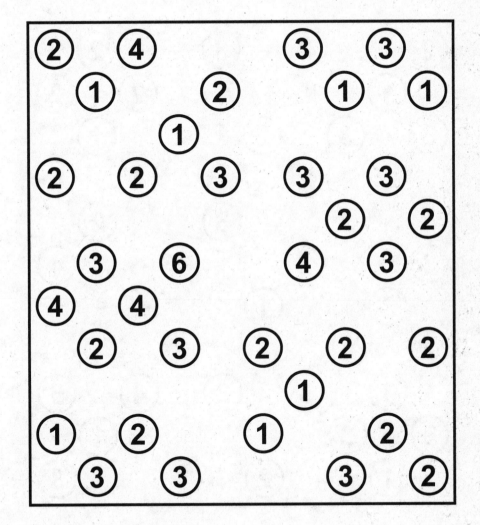

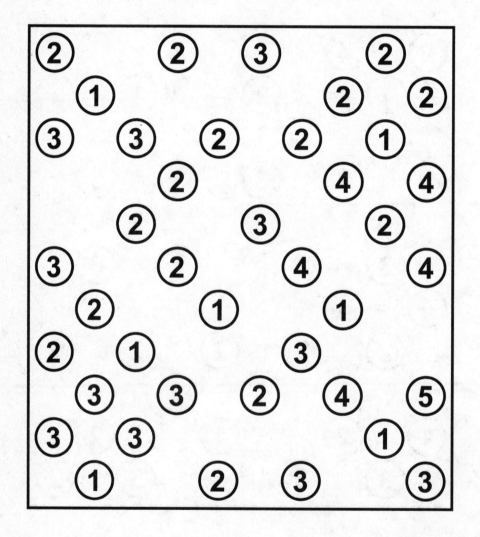

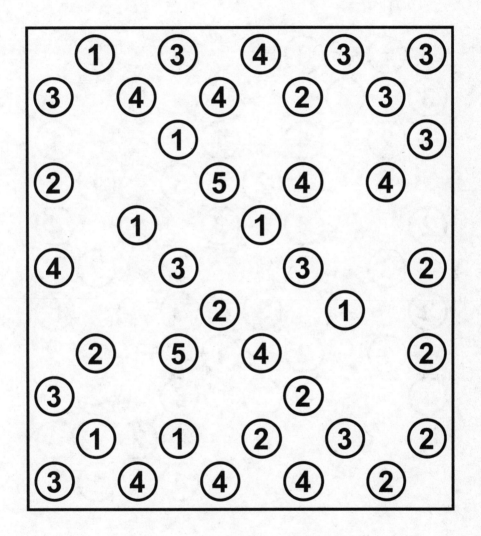

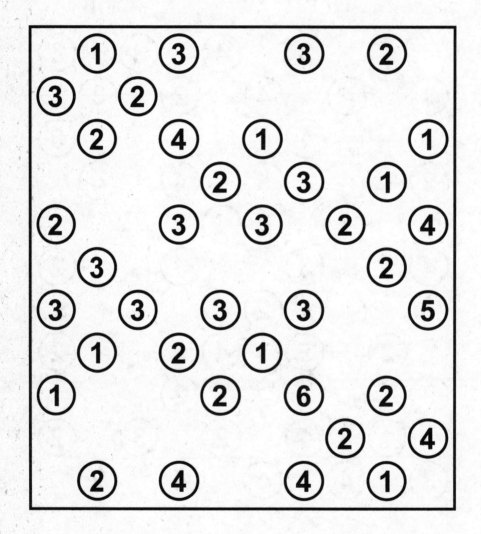

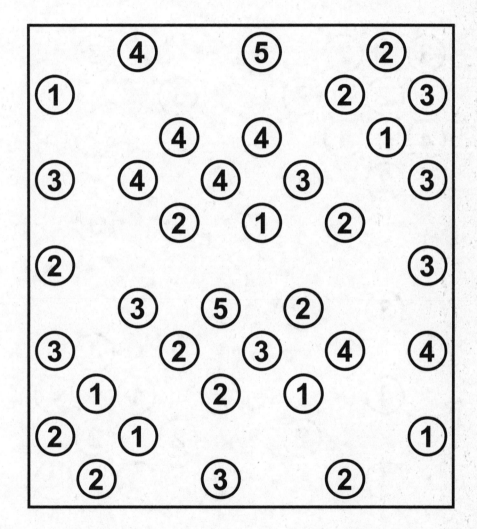

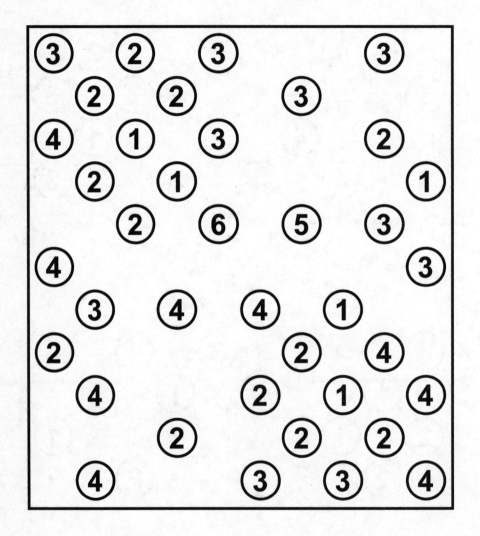

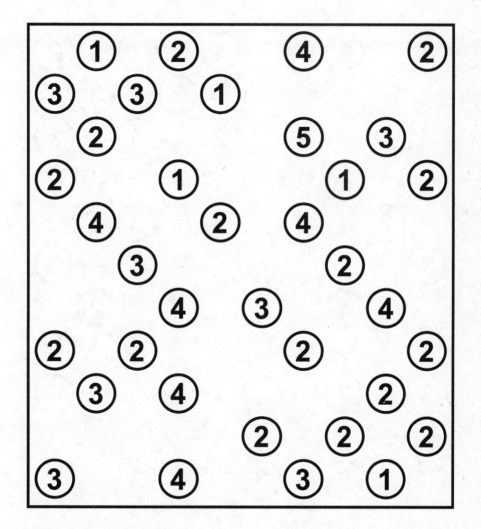

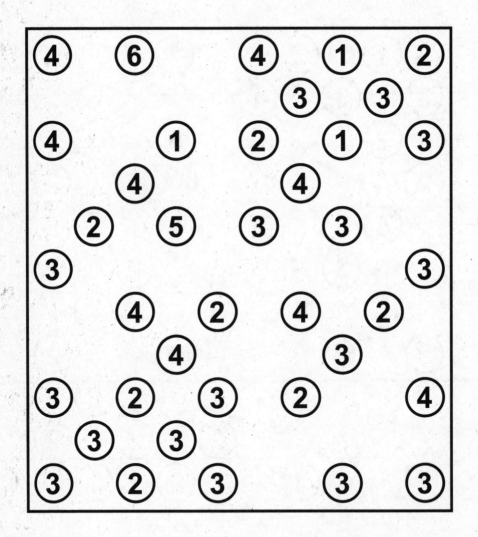

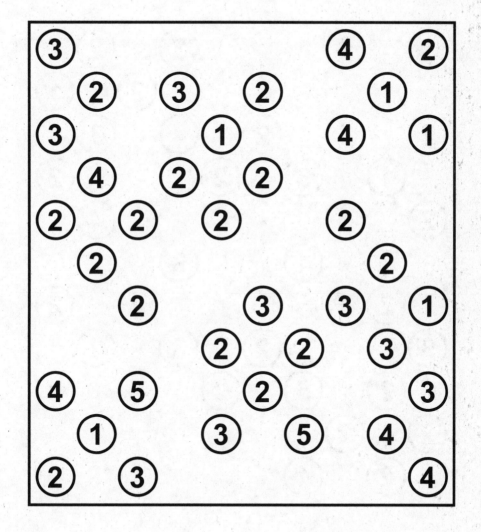

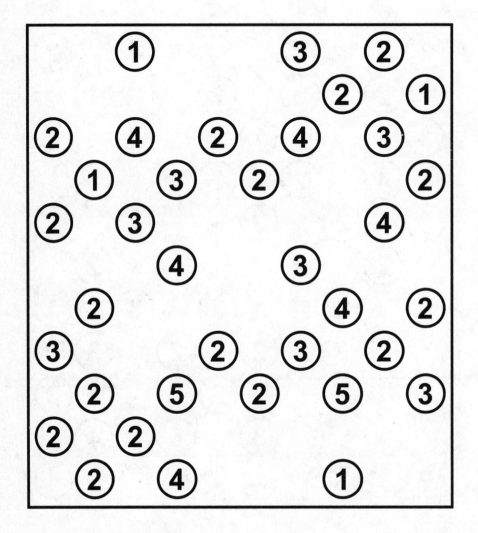

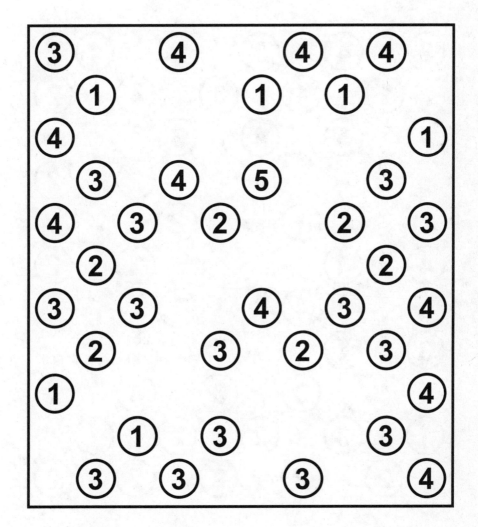

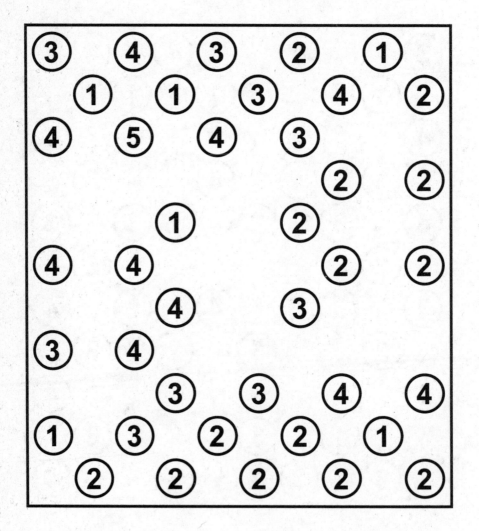

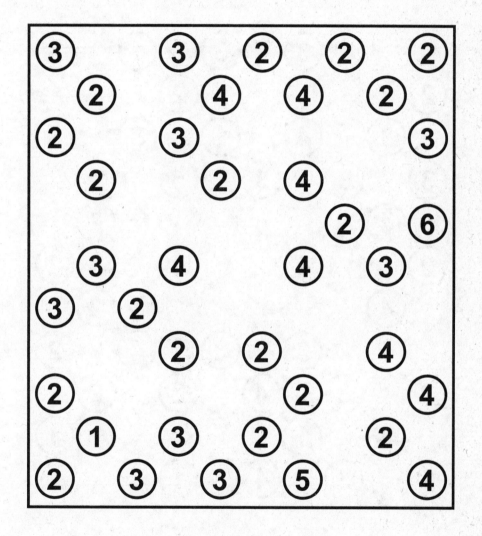

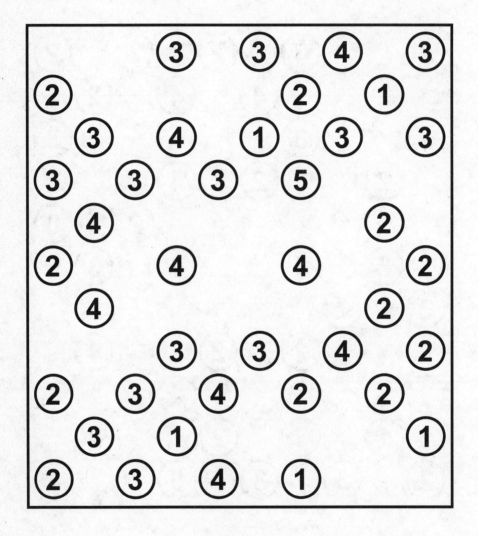

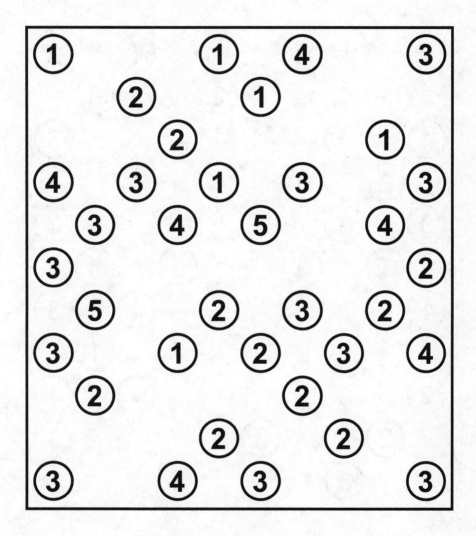

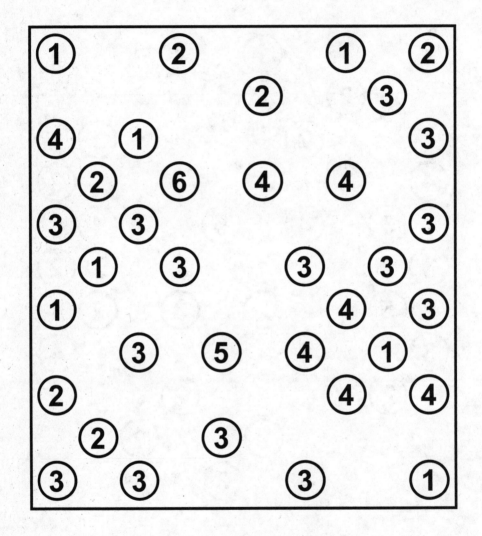

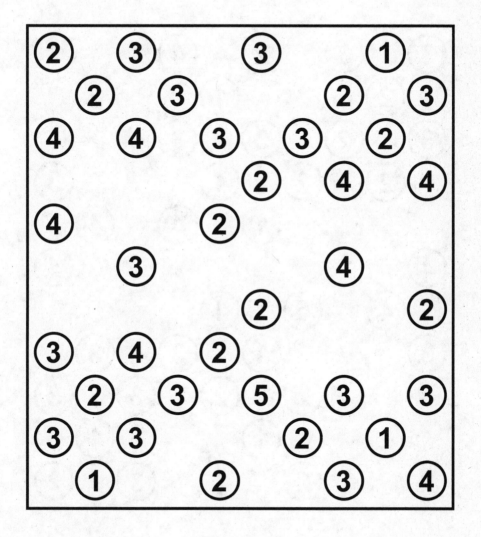

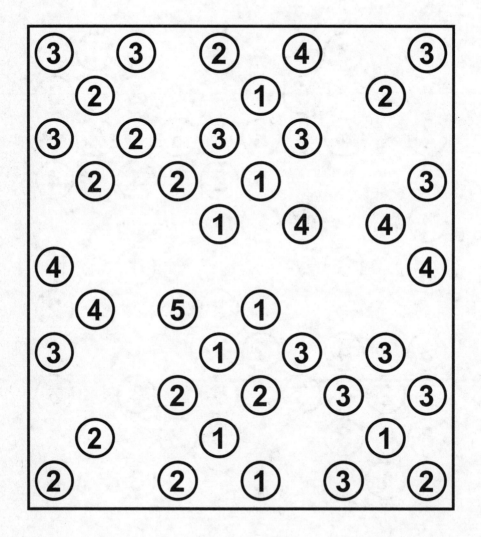

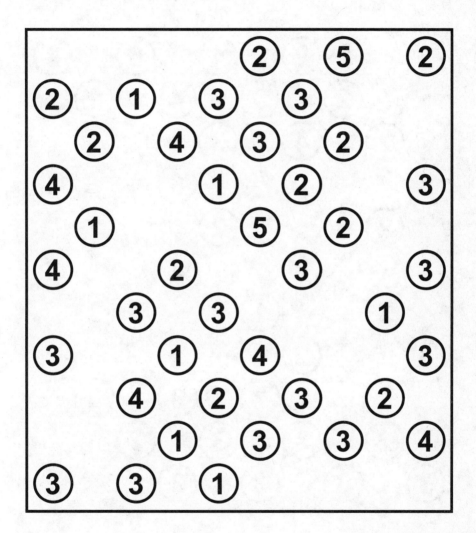

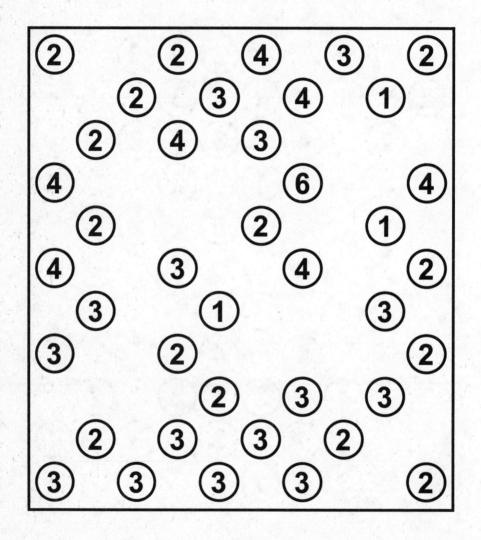

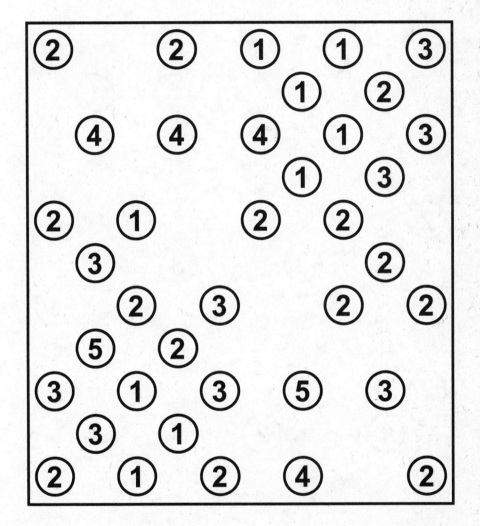

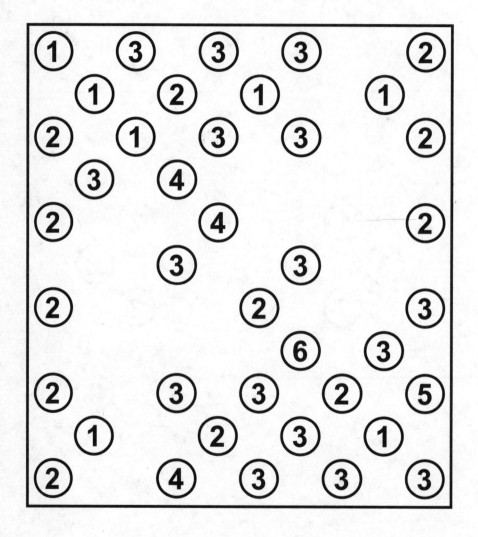

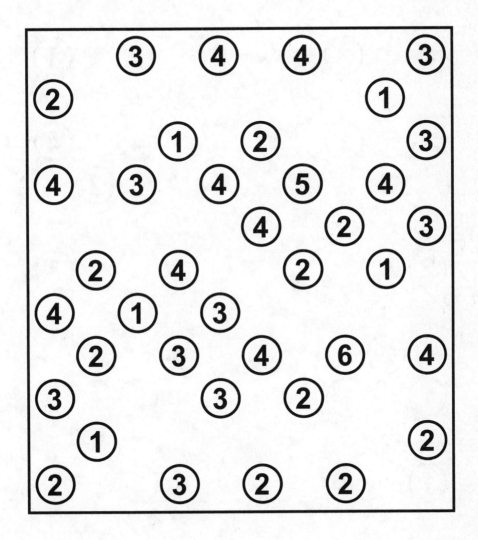

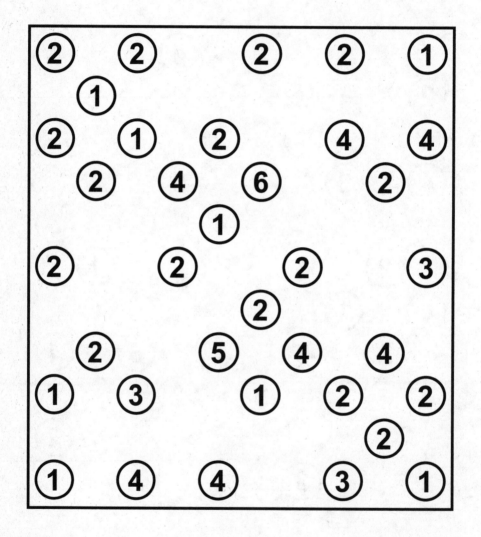

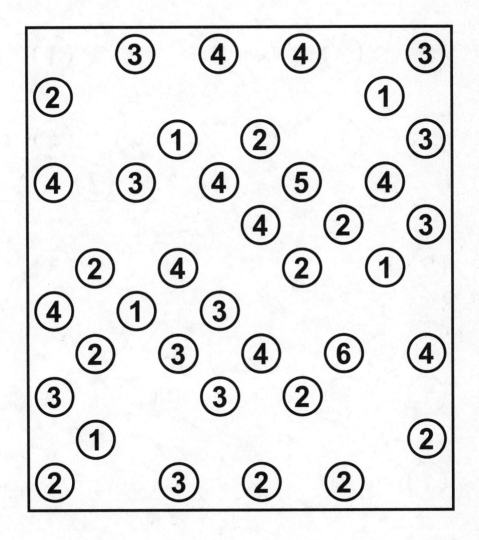

② ② ② ② ①
  ①
② ① ② ④ ④
  ② ④ ⑥ ②
      ①
② ② ② ③
      ②
  ② ⑤ ④ ④
① ③ ① ② ②
          ②
① ④ ④ ③ ①

# LEVEL 3 | MALICIOUS

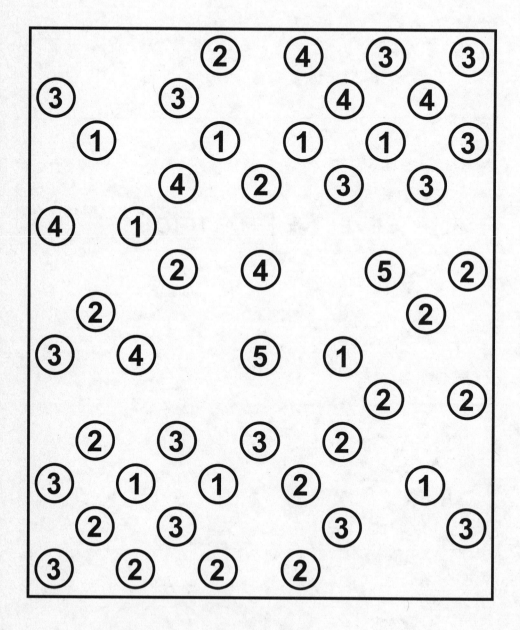

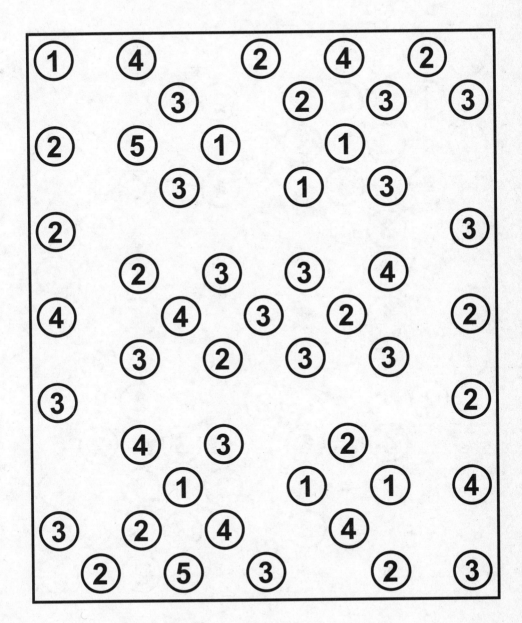

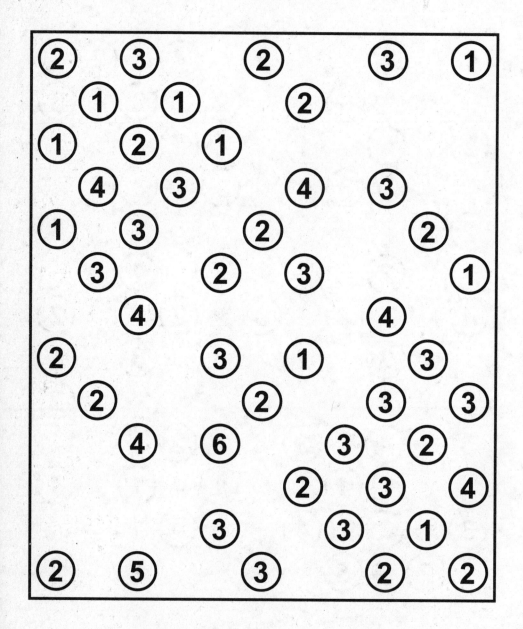

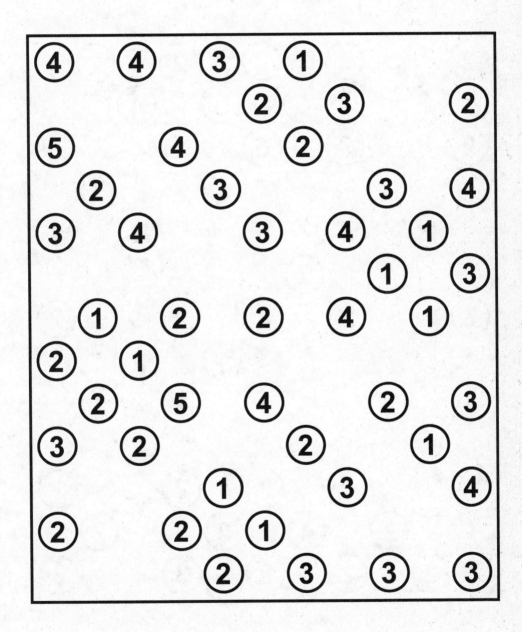

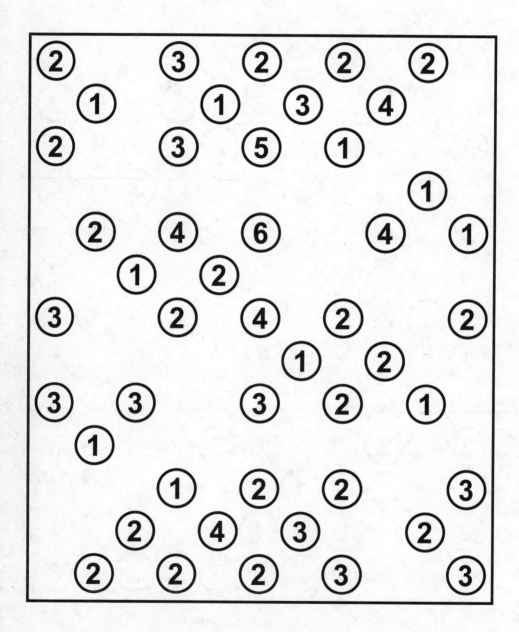

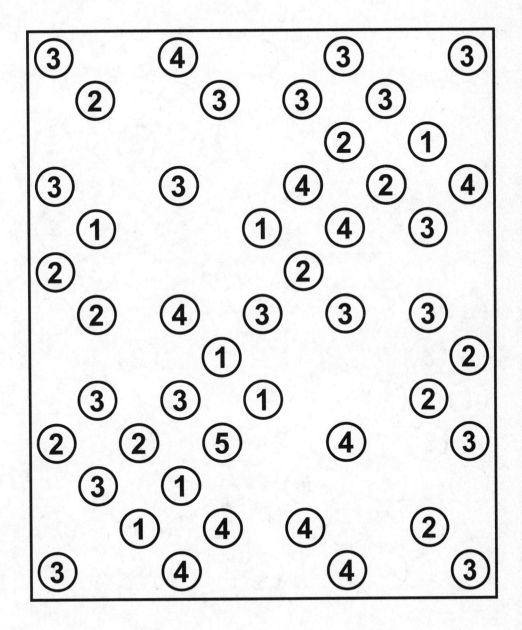

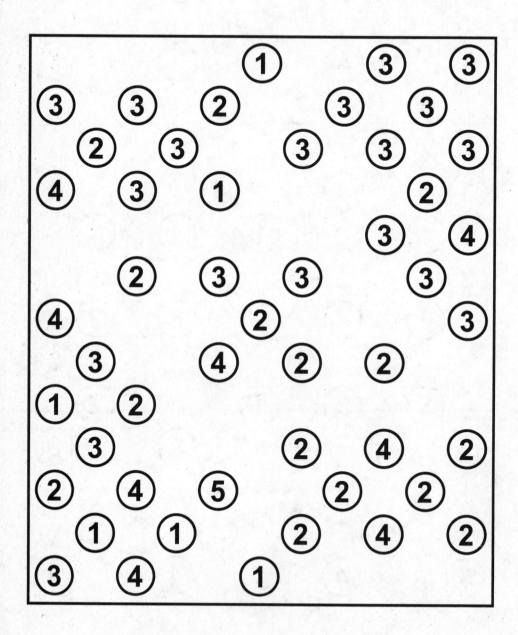

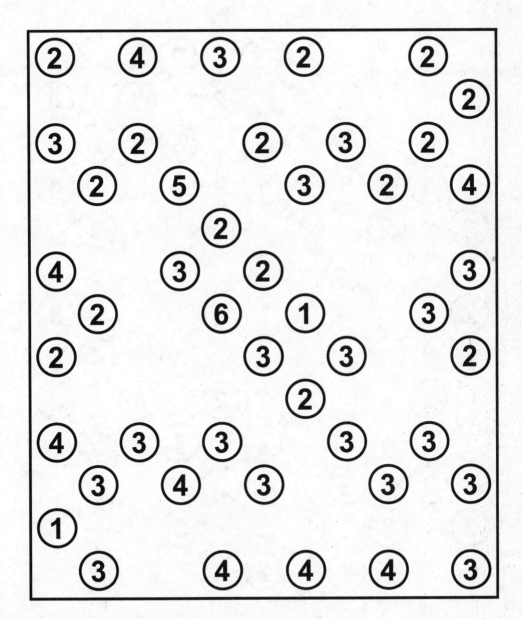

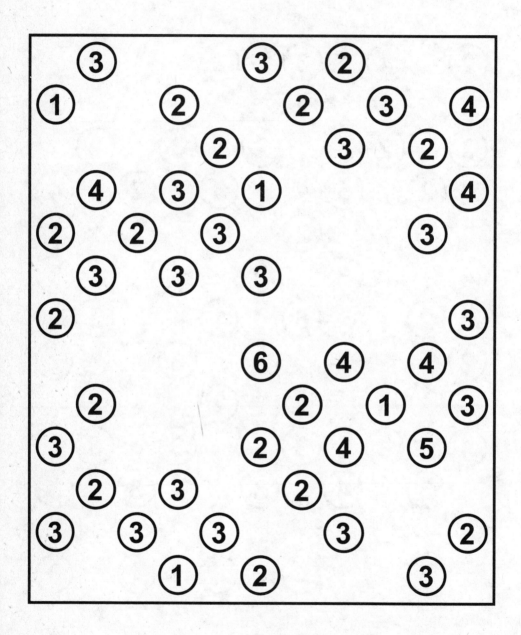

② ② ① ② ③

② ③ ①

②

② ③ ④ ③ ③

③ ④ ④ ② ①

① ③

③ ⑤ ⑤ ③ ①

② ①

② ② ④ ③ ④

③ ② ④ ③ ④

②

① ② ④

④ ④ ③ ① ①

①  ②③
②    ②    ②①①
  ①②    ③③
    ①    ①②③
③②      ①
    ④③①
③    ③①④      ③
    ①③②
      ②      ③④
③④①    ②
②④    ③③
①②②    ④    ④
④⑤    ①

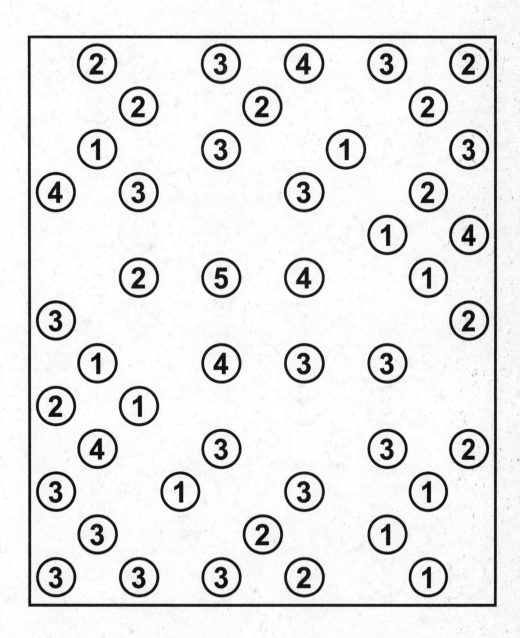

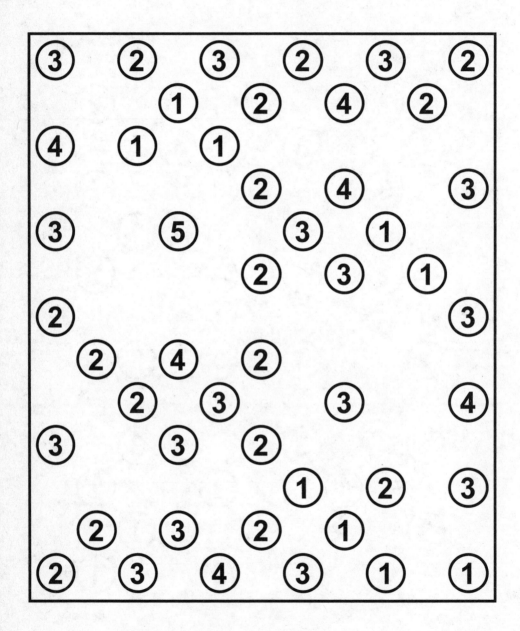

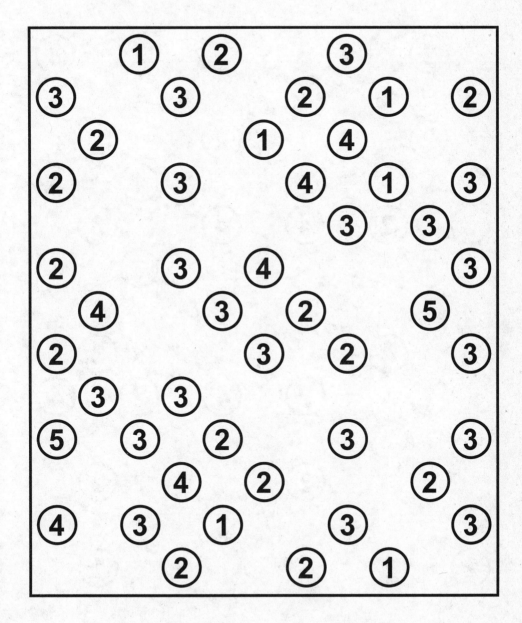

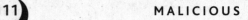
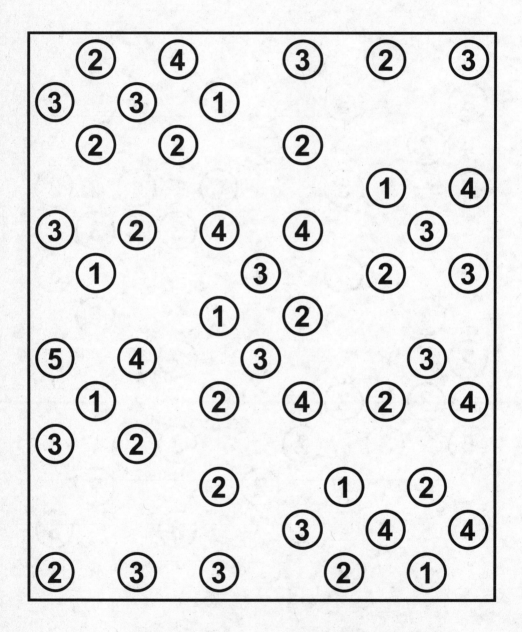

②　②　　③　④　②

　　　　　　①　　①

　①　　②　　③　②

④　②　　③

　①　③　　　②

④　③　　⑤　③　　③

　②　　　　　②

②　　④　④　　②　④

　③　　　　①　①

　　　②　　②　④

　③　④　③　　①

①　①

　②　③　③　　④　④

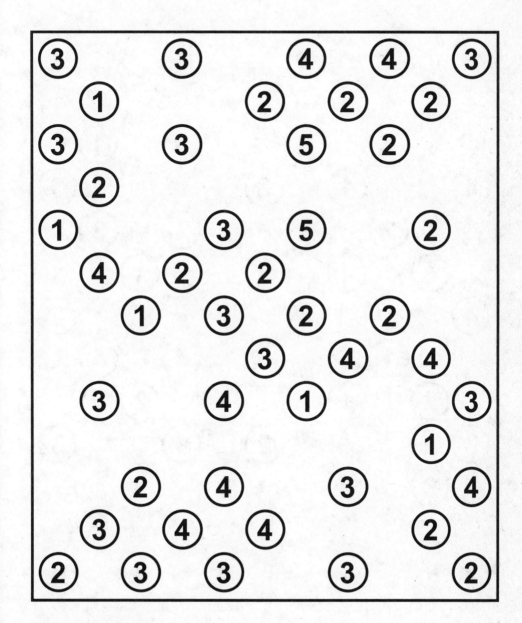

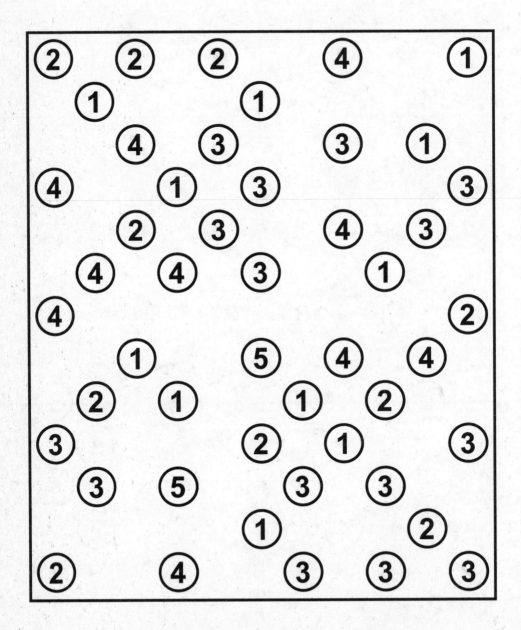

| | | | | | | | | | | |
|---|---|---|---|---|---|---|---|---|---|---|
| 3 | | 4 | | | 3 | | 2 | | | 3 |
| | | | | 1 | | | | | 2 | |
| 4 | | | 4 | | | 3 | | 2 | | 3 |
| | | | | | 2 | | | | 4 | |
| 3 | | | 4 | | | 2 | | | | 3 |
| | 1 | | | | 2 | | 4 | | 4 | |
| 3 | | | | | | | | | | 3 |
| | 4 | | 4 | | 5 | | | | 1 | |
| 1 | | | | 1 | | | 3 | | | 2 |
| | 3 | | | | 1 | | | | | |
| 1 | | 2 | | 4 | | | 3 | | | 3 |
| | 2 | | | | | 1 | | | | |
| 2 | | | 3 | | 3 | | | 3 | | 3 |

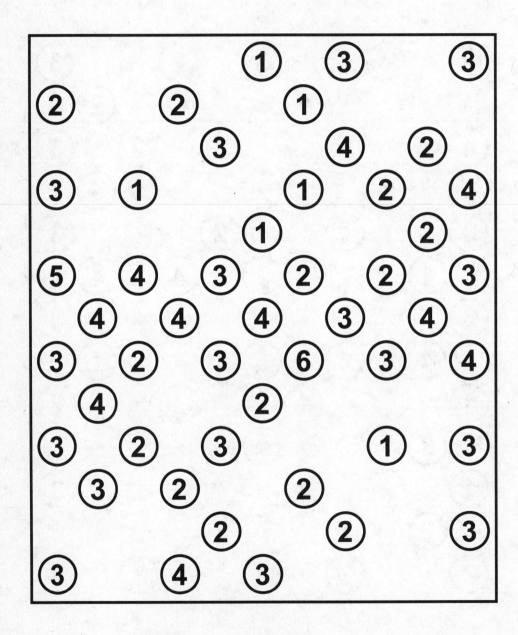

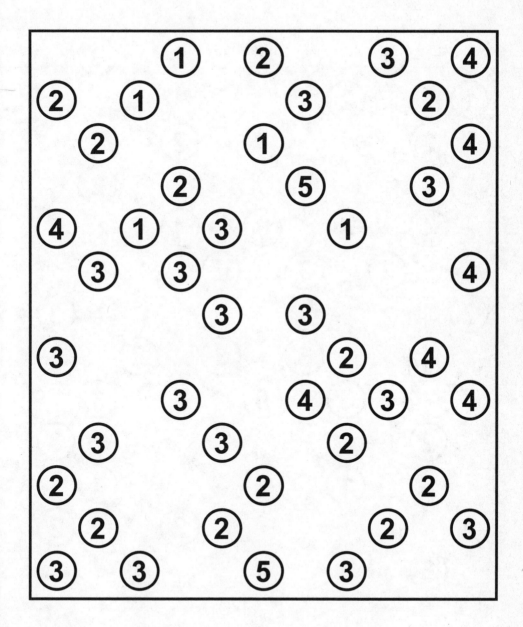

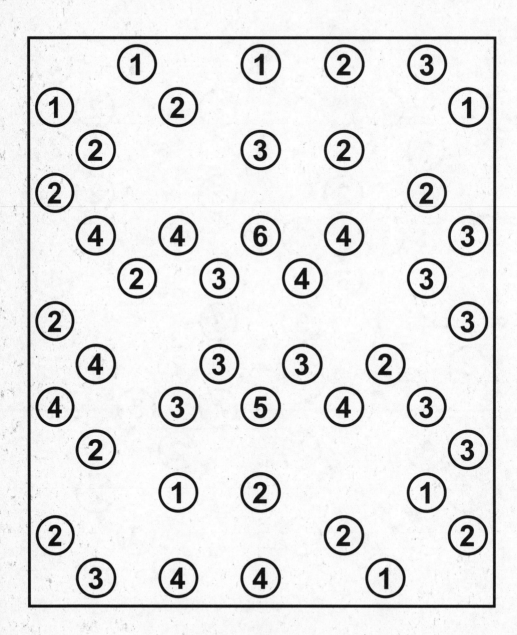

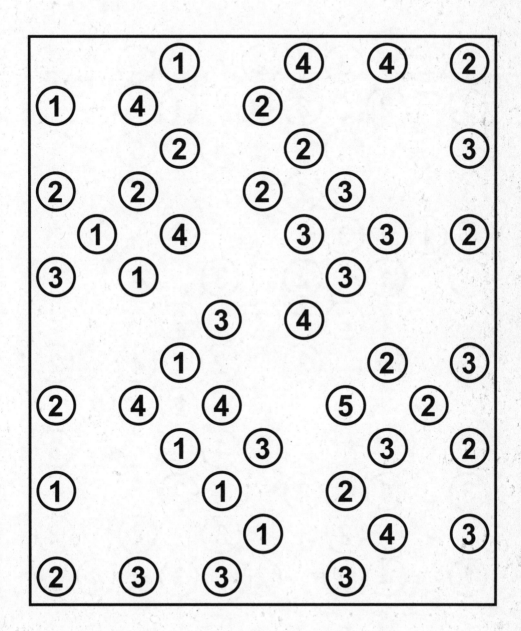

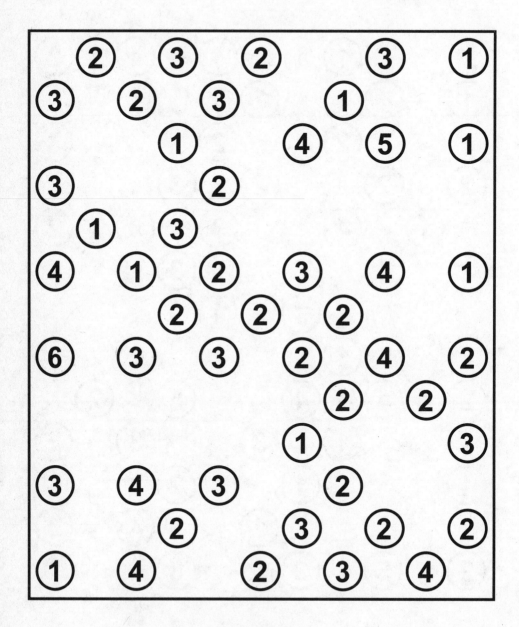

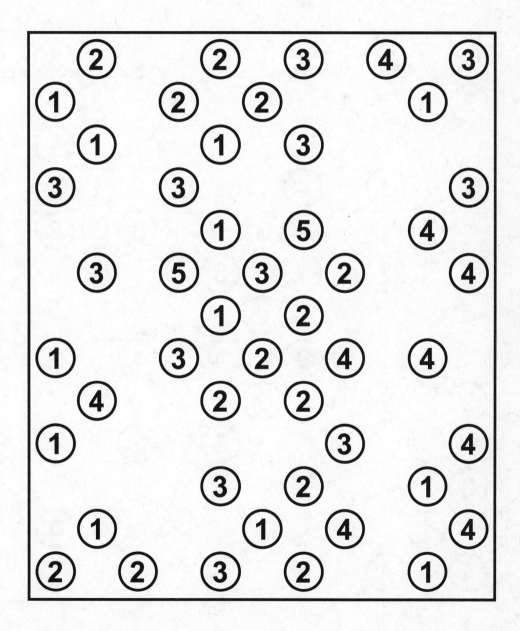

④ ③ ③ ③

② ① ③ ③

①

④ ① ④ ② ①

③ ③ ②

④ ② ③ ③ ①

②

① ② ④ ① ②

③ ① ①

③ ⑤ ⑤ ② ④

③

① ② ② ④

④ ④ ③ ③

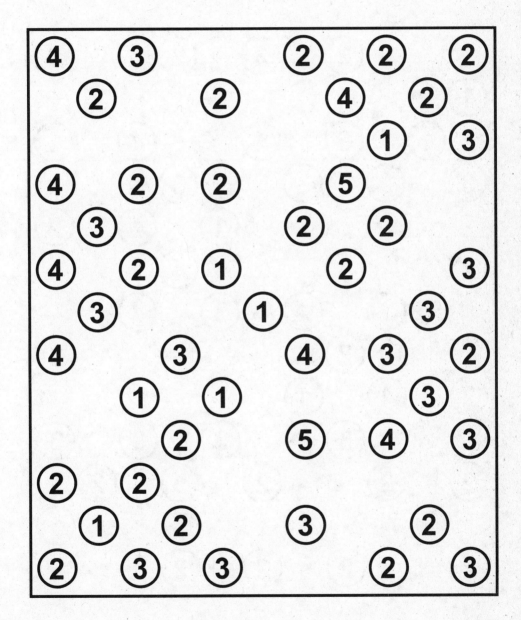

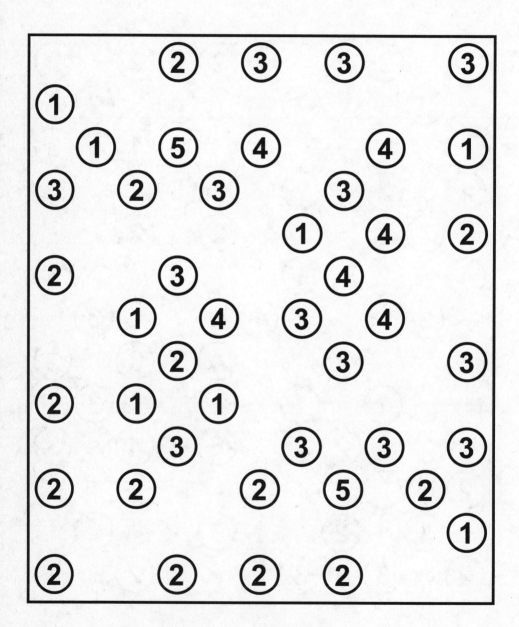

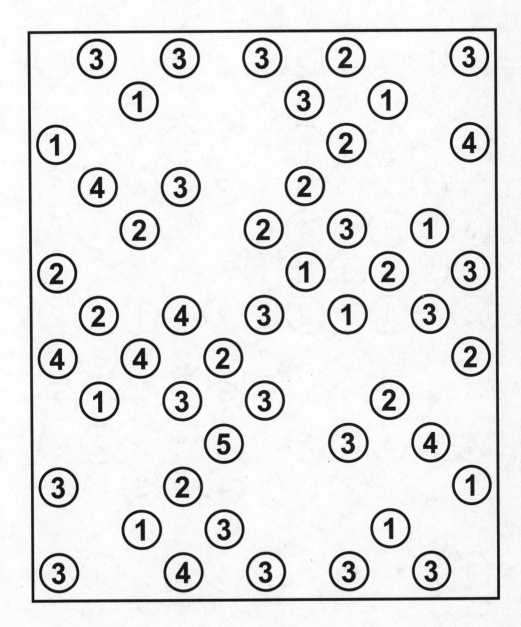

| | | | | | | | | | | |
|---|---|---|---|---|---|---|---|---|---|---|
| | 2 | | | 5 | | | 4 | | | 2 |
| | | | | | | | | 2 | | |
| 2 | | 2 | | 5 | | | 3 | | | |
| | 2 | | | | | 2 | | 4 | | 3 |
| 3 | | 4 | | 4 | | | 2 | | 3 | |
| | 2 | | 3 | | 1 | | | | | |
| 3 | | 1 | | 2 | | 2 | | 1 | | 2 |
| | | | | | 2 | | 2 | | 3 | |
| | 1 | | 3 | | | 3 | | 4 | | 3 |
| 4 | | 3 | | 2 | | | | | 2 | |
| | | | 2 | | | 4 | | 3 | | 2 |
| | | 1 | | | | | | | | |
| 3 | | | 3 | | | 4 | | | 3 | |

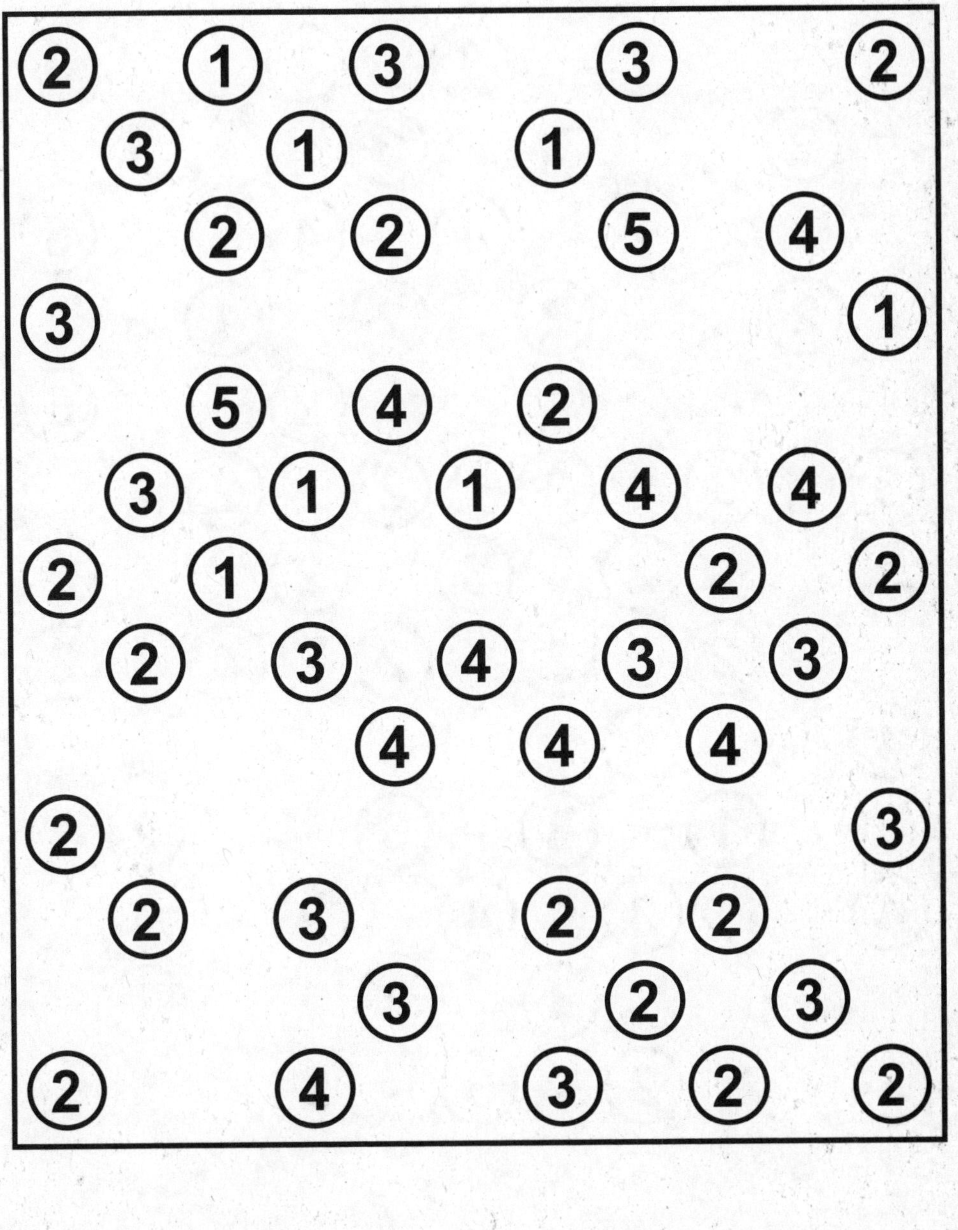

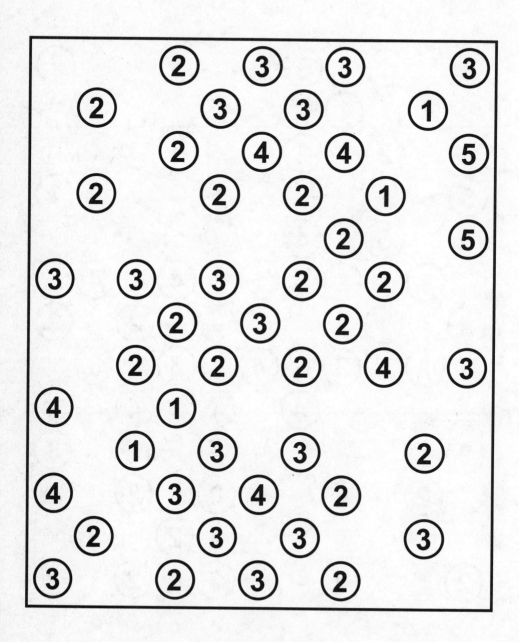

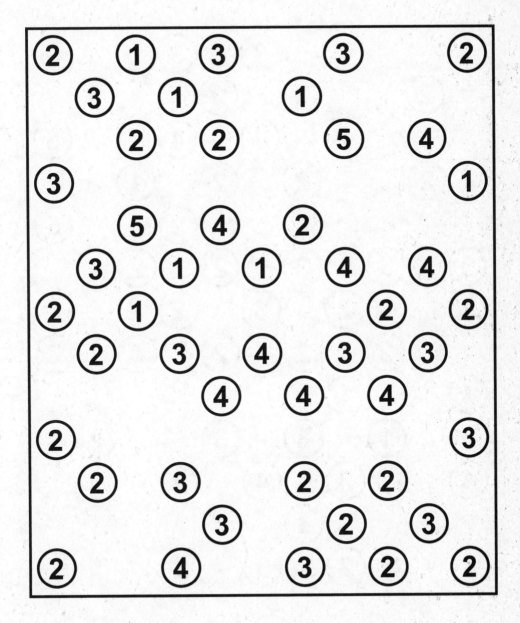

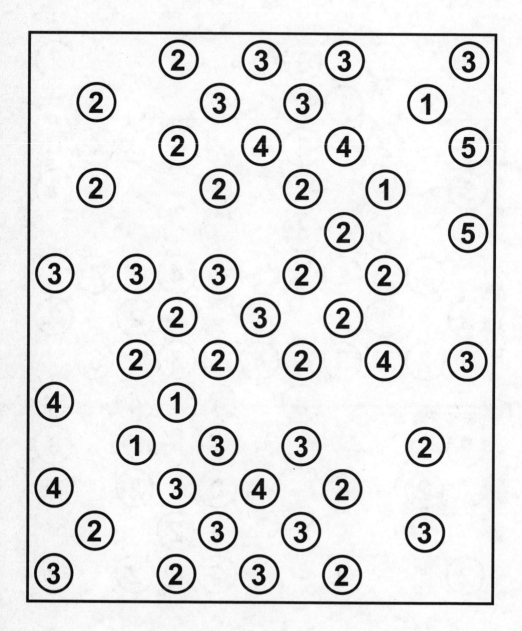

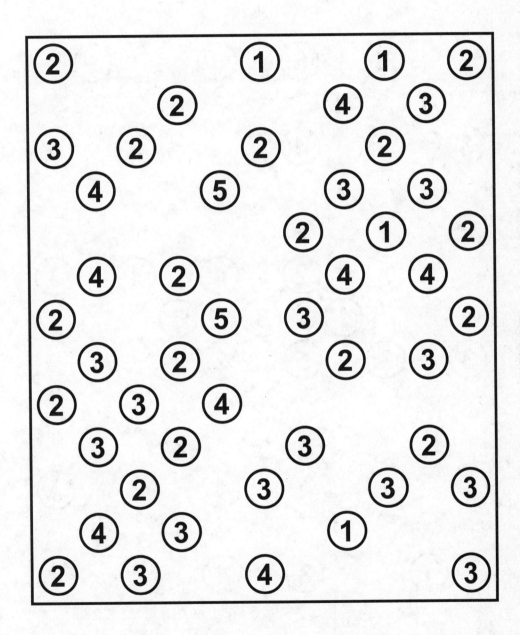

(2) (3) (6) (3) (1)
(1) (2)
(3) (2) (4) (3) (1)
(2) (3) (4)
(2) (1)
(3) (2) (4) (4) (3)
(1) (3) (3)
(3) (3) (5) (2) (1)
(1) (1)
(4) (3) (3)
(1) (1) (4) (2) (1)
(1) (2)
(1) (3) (4) (2) (2)

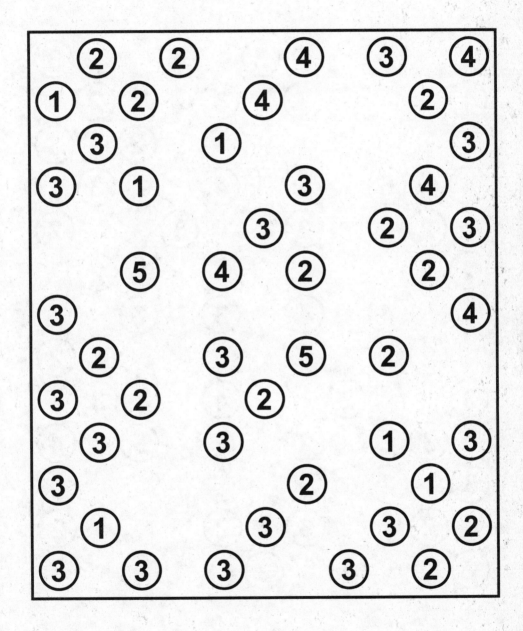

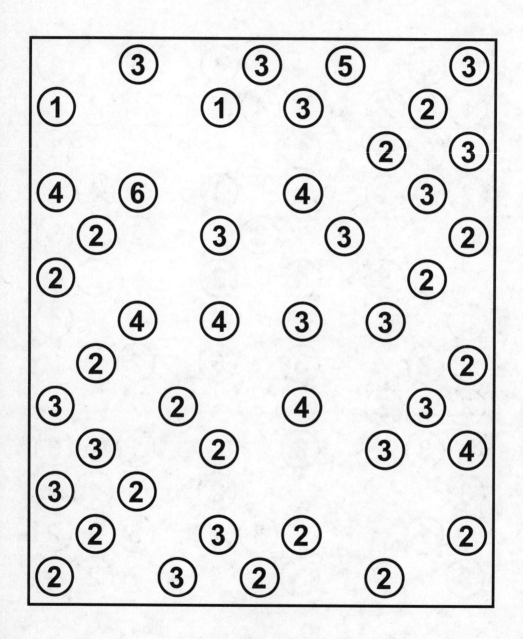

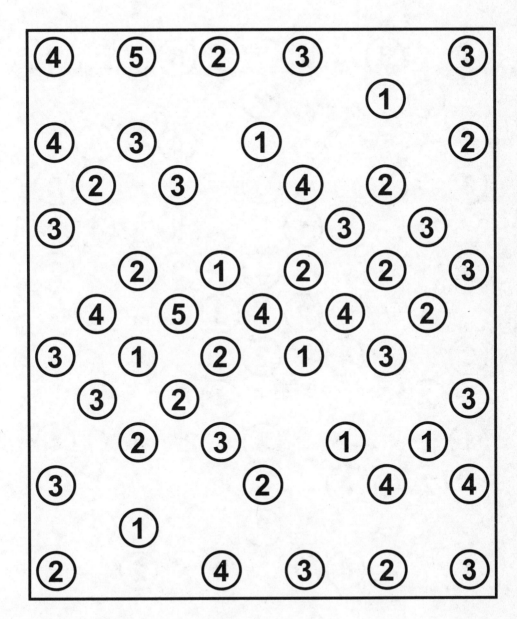

④ ③ ② ③ ③
② ②
④ ③
③ ② ③ ③
③ ① ④
③ ③ ④ ③ ②
③ ② ③ ③
③ ④ ② ④ ⑤
② ① ①
① ③ ④ ④
② ④
② ②
① ④ ③ ② ③

| | | | | | | | | | | |
|---|---|---|---|---|---|---|---|---|---|---|
| 1 | | | 3 | | | | 3 | | | 2 |
| | | 2 | | | 3 | | | | 2 | |
| | | | | | | | | | | 2 |
| 2 | | 4 | | | 2 | | 1 | | 3 | |
| | | | 2 | | | 3 | | 2 | | 2 |
| 2 | | 3 | | | 3 | | 1 | | | |
| | 2 | | | | | | | | 1 | |
| | | | 1 | | 4 | | | 4 | | 2 |
| 2 | | 3 | | 3 | | | 1 | | | |
| | 5 | | 4 | | 4 | | | 6 | | 3 |
| 3 | | | | | | | | | | |
| | 1 | | | | 1 | | | 1 | | |
| 4 | | | 4 | | | | 2 | | | 1 |

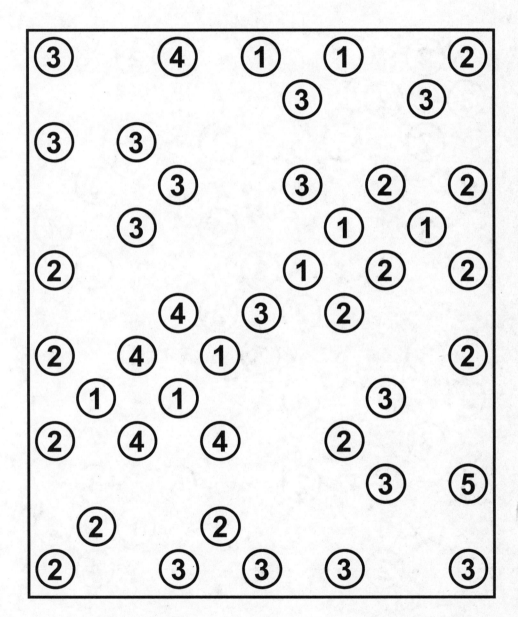

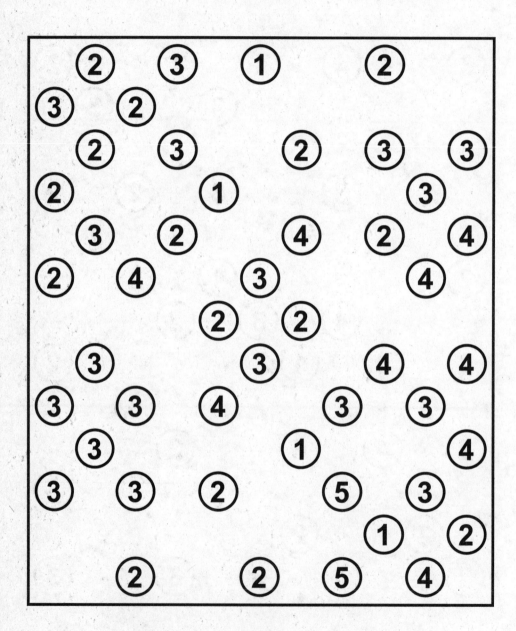

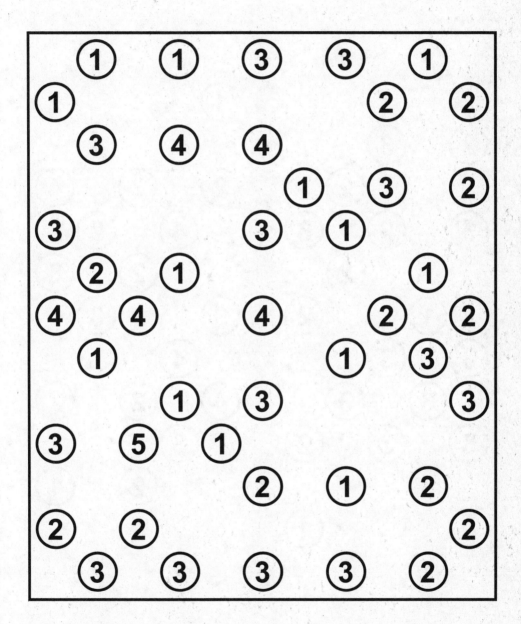

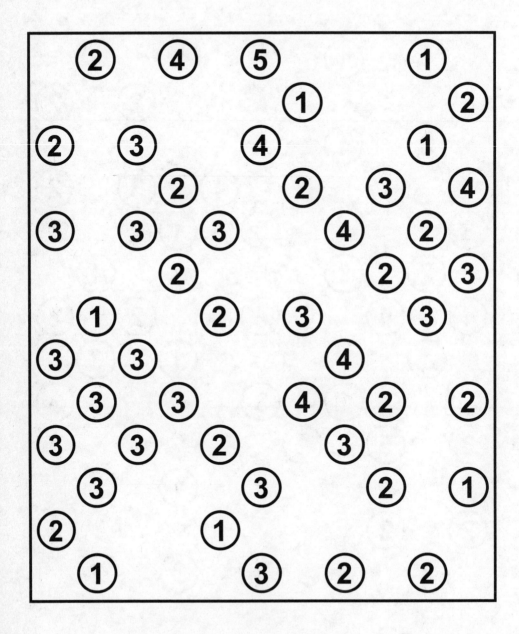

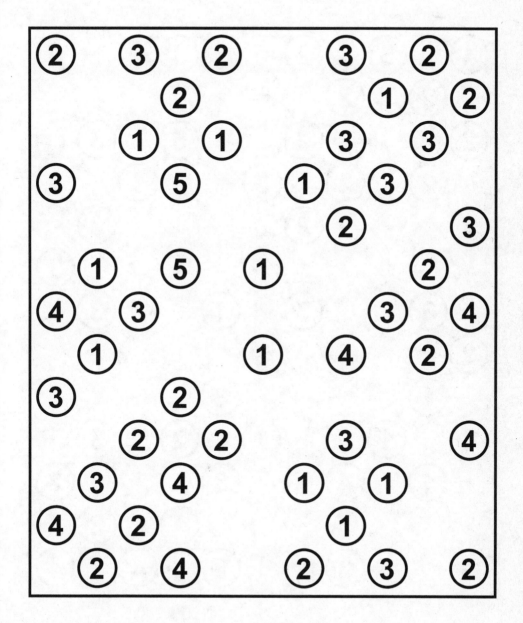

④ ③ ② ③ ④

② ②

② ② ⑤ ③

② ② ③ ① ③

① ② ③

⑤ ④ ③

③ ③ ① ③

② ② ③

① ③ ②

③ ① ① ② ③

① ④ ③ ②

① ②

② ③ ② ④ ④

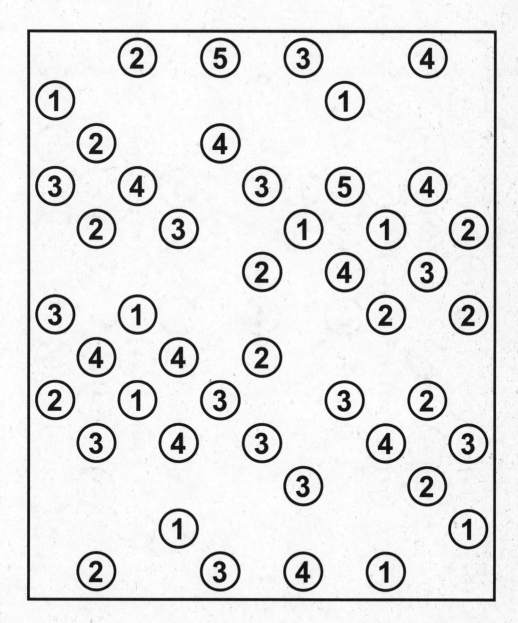

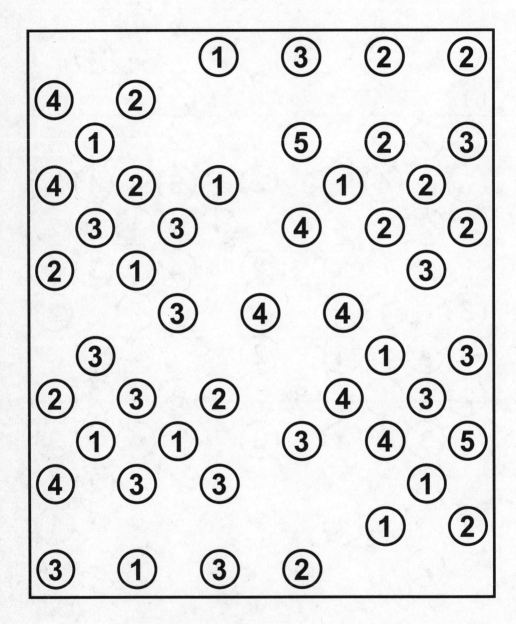

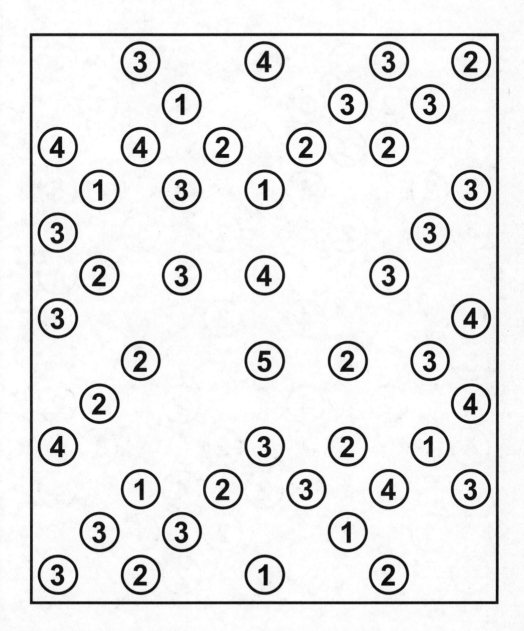

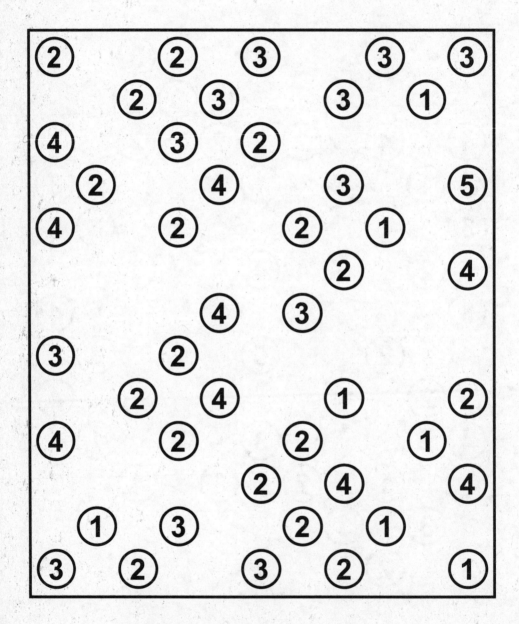

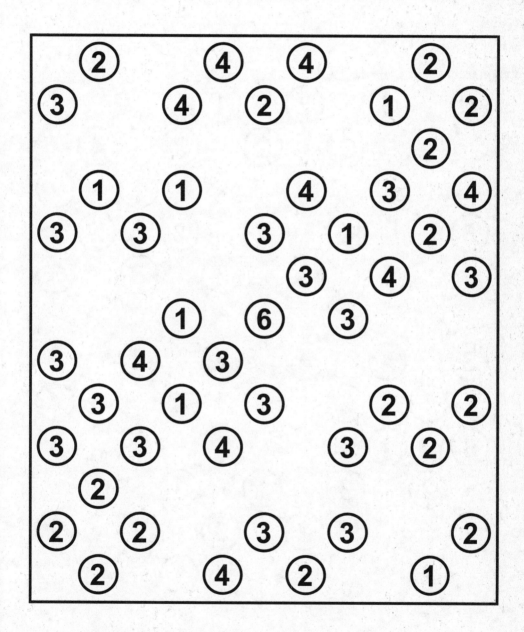

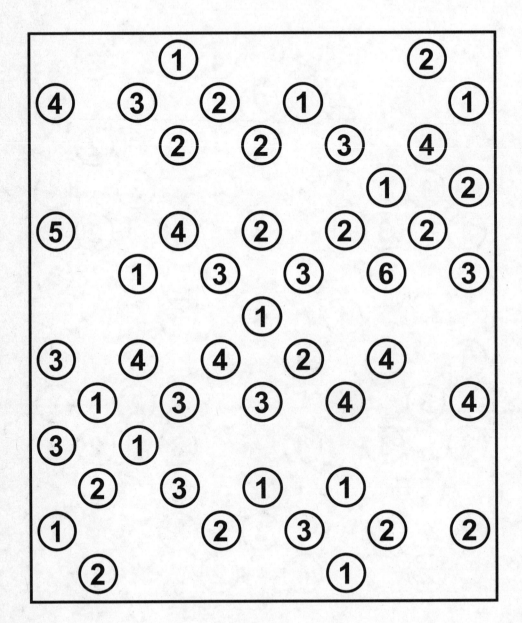

150

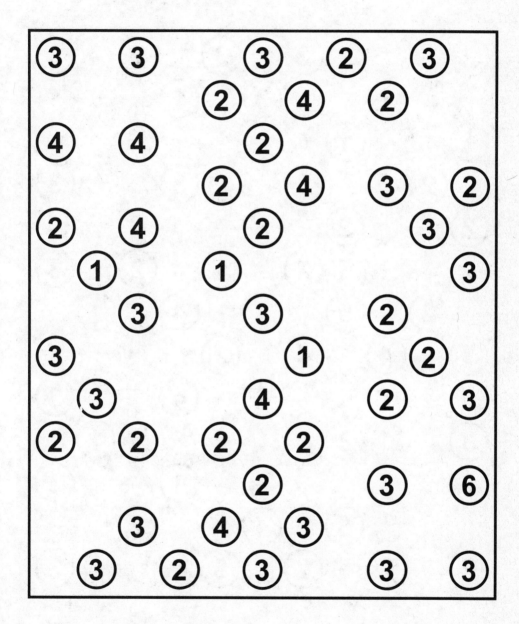

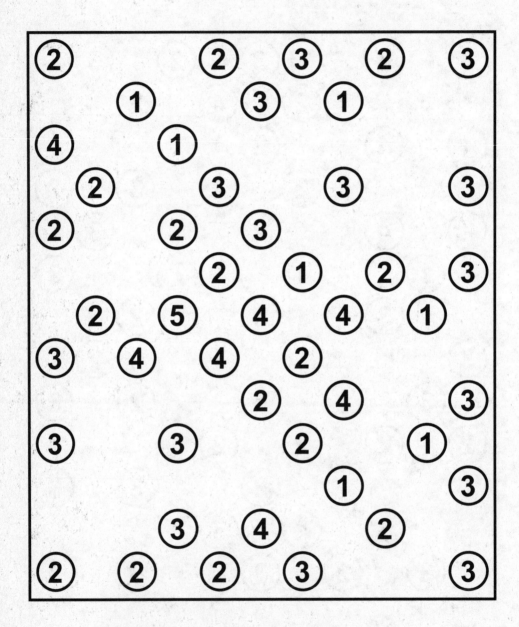

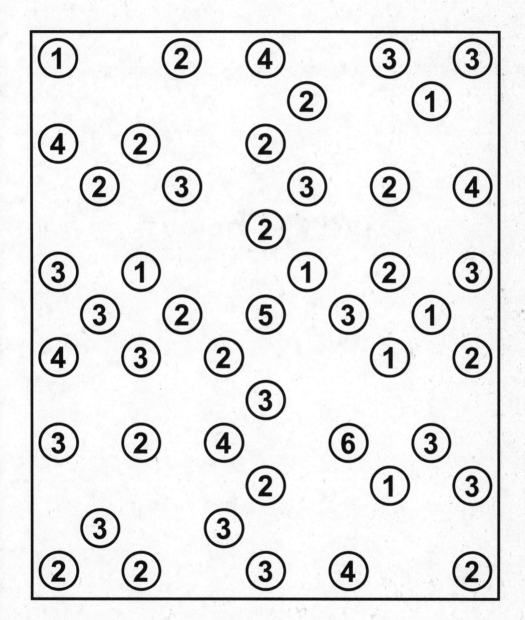

LEVEL 4 | VICIOUS

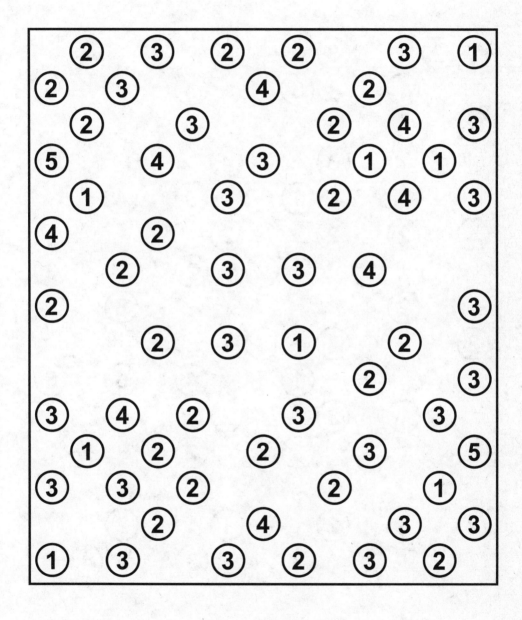

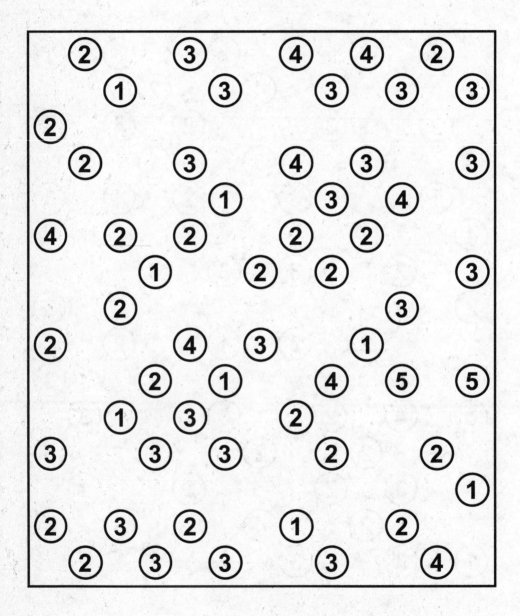

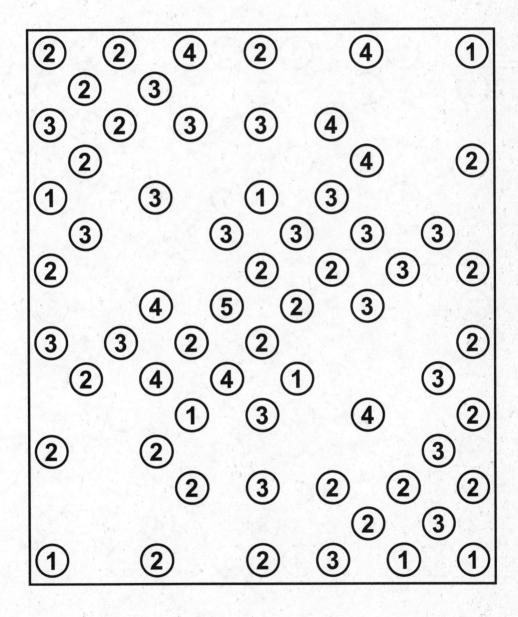

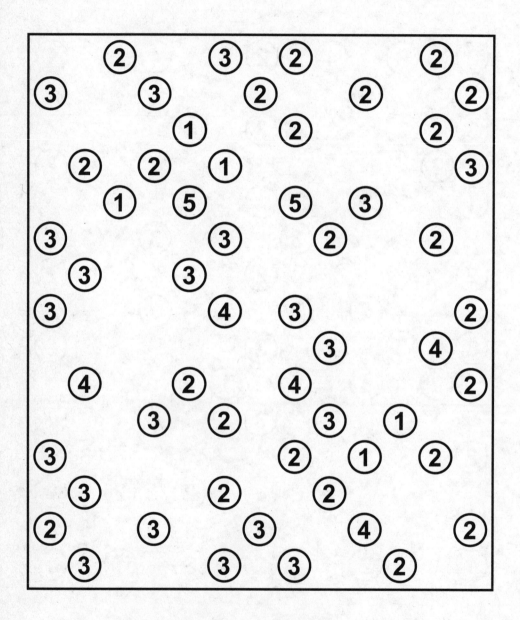

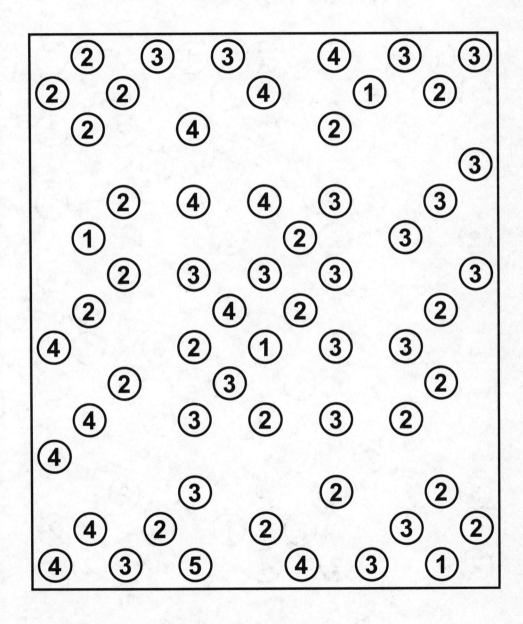

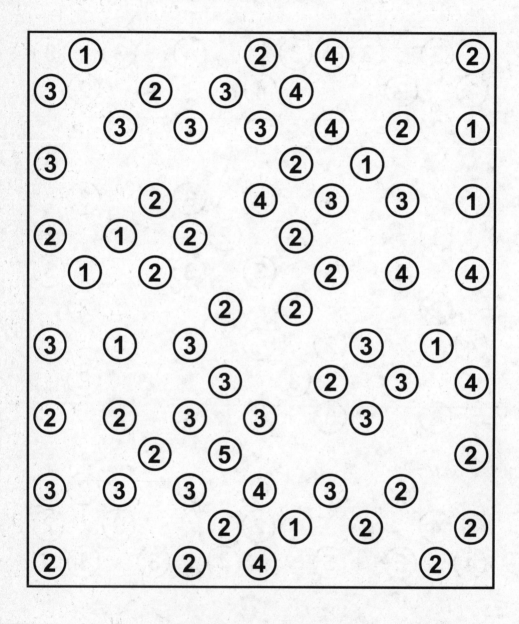

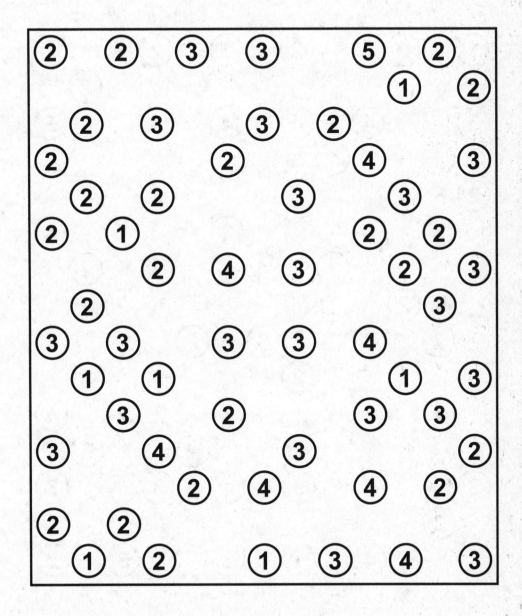

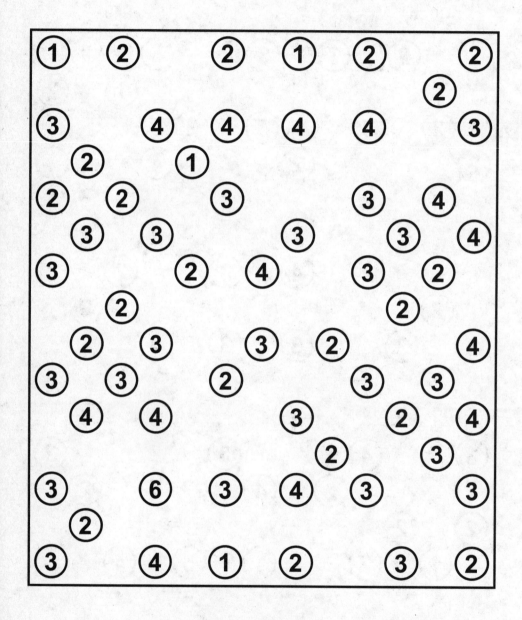

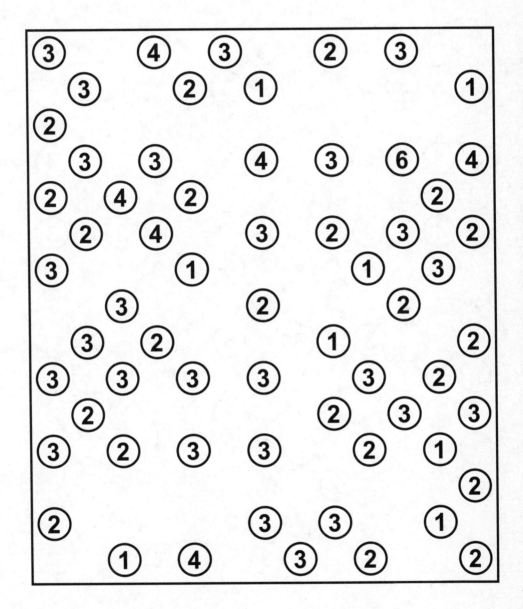

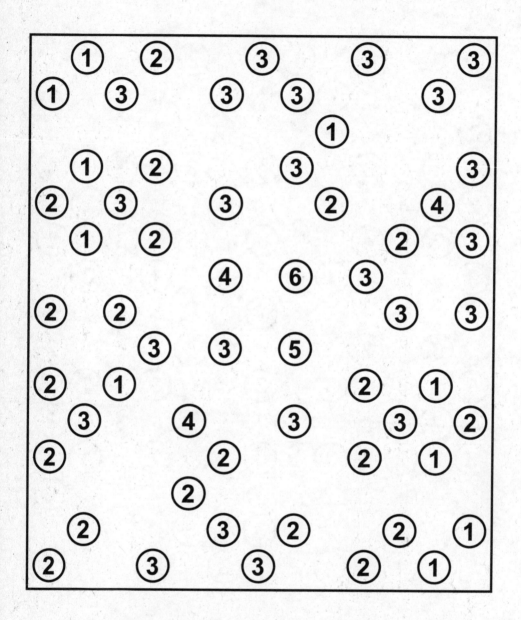

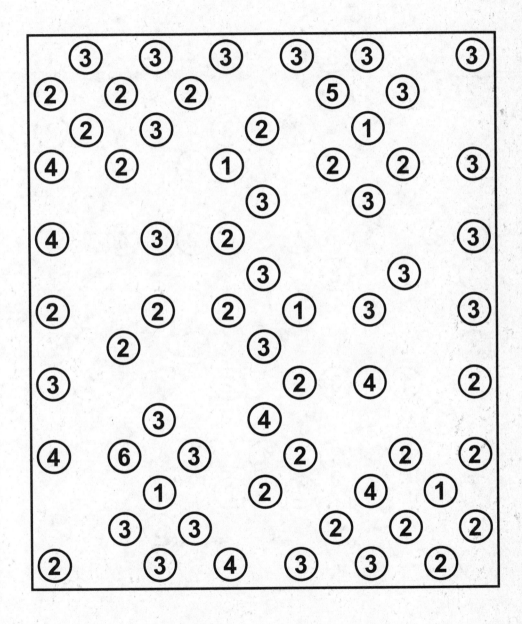

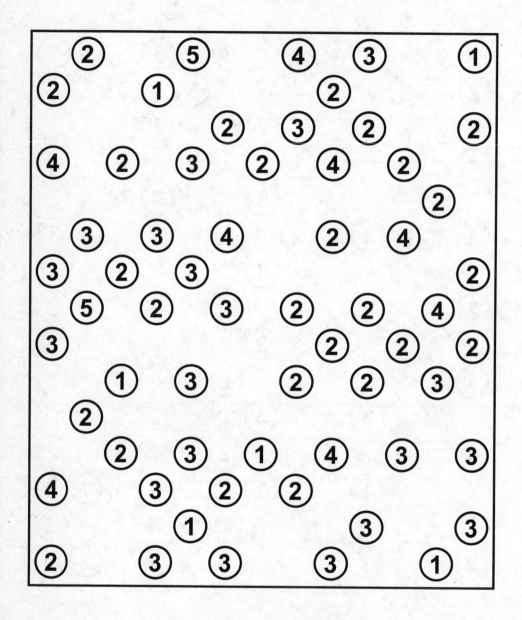

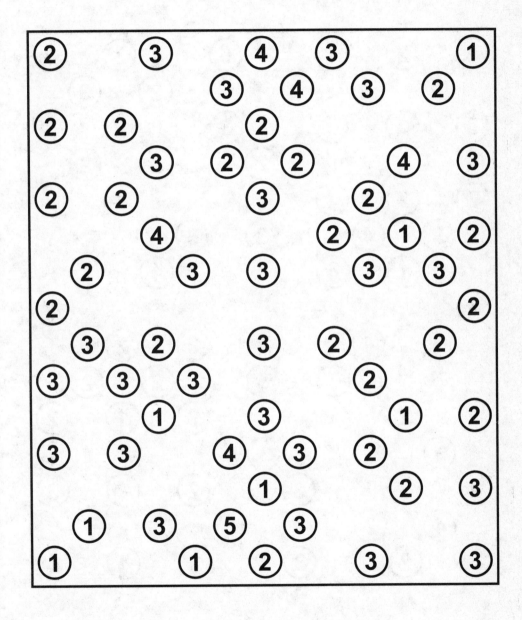

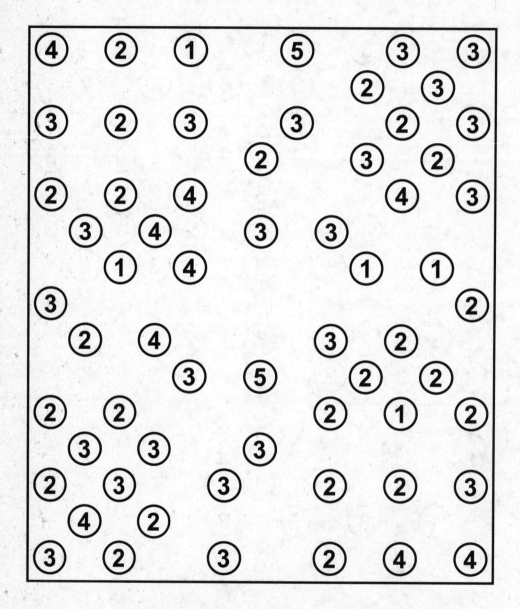

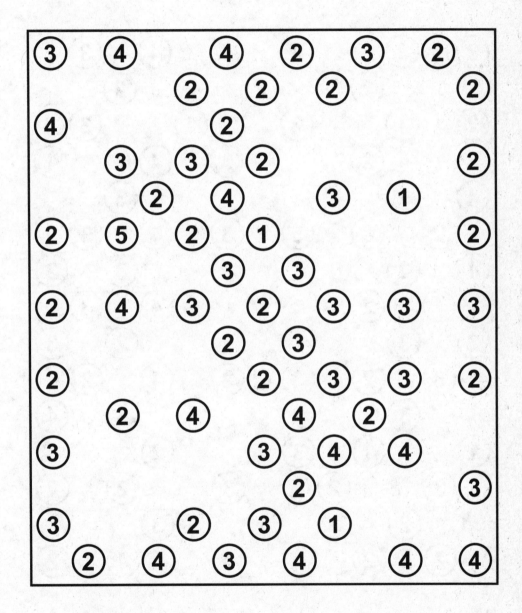

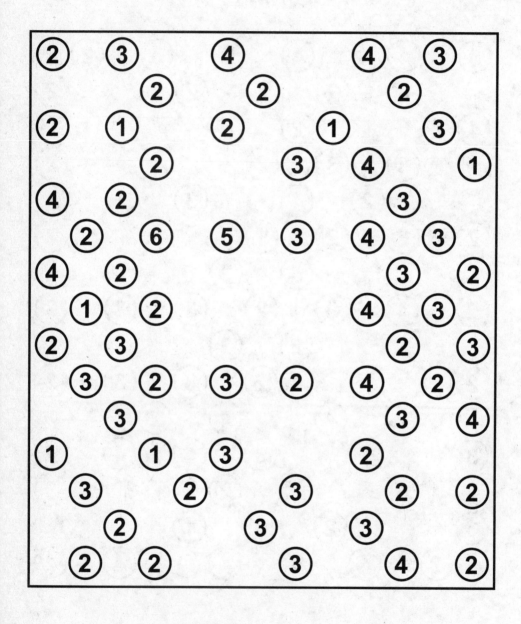

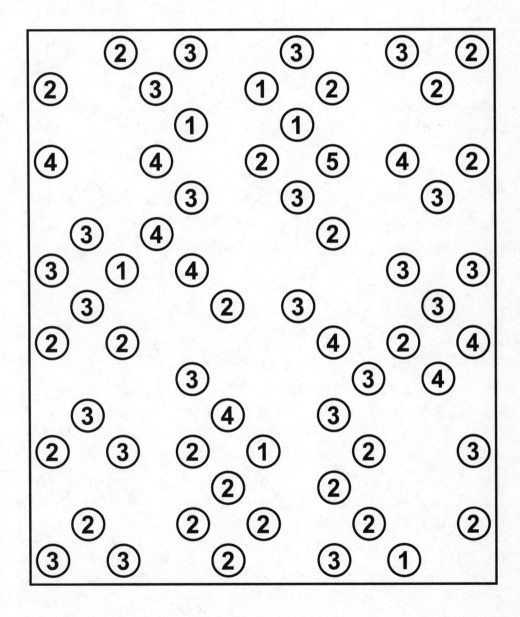

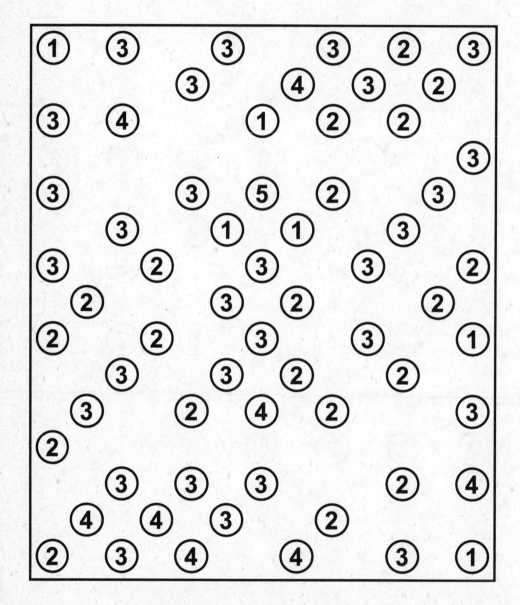

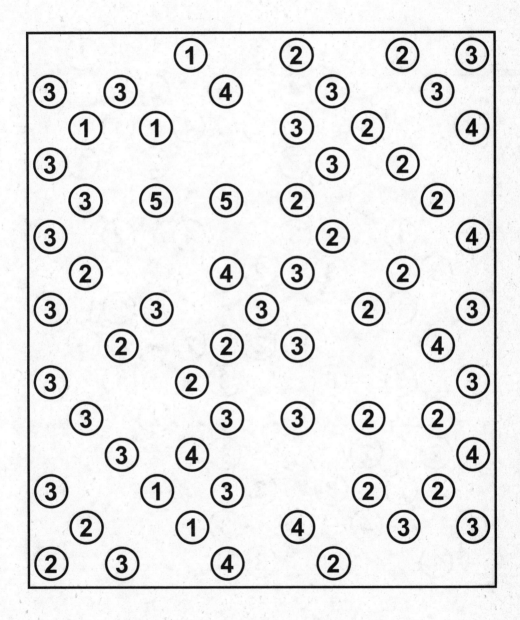

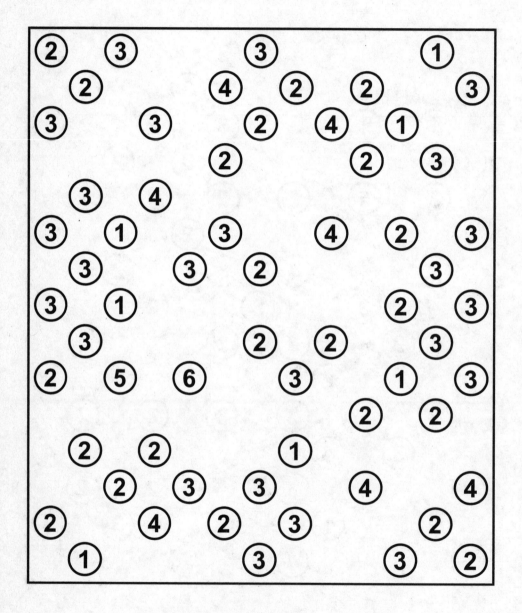

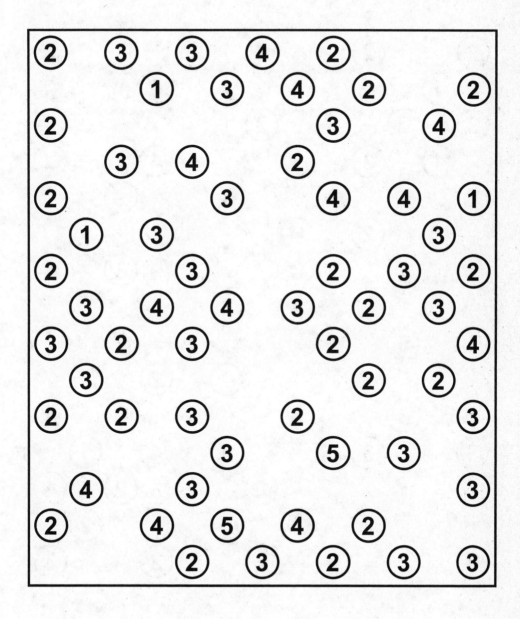

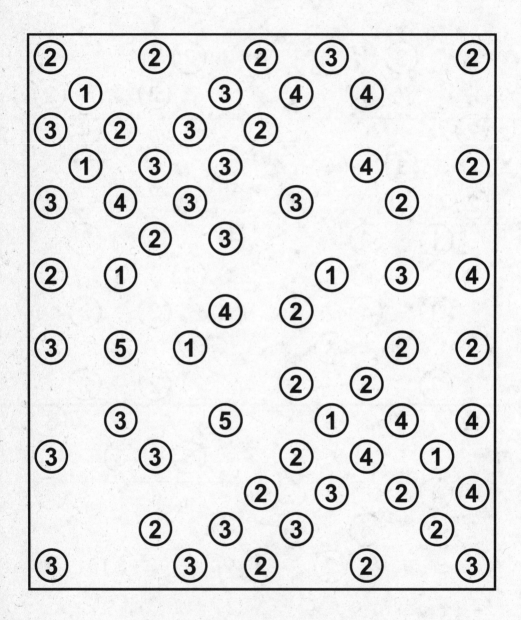

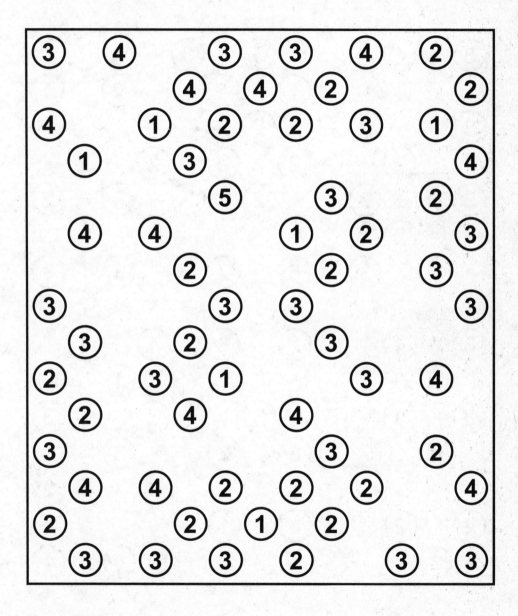

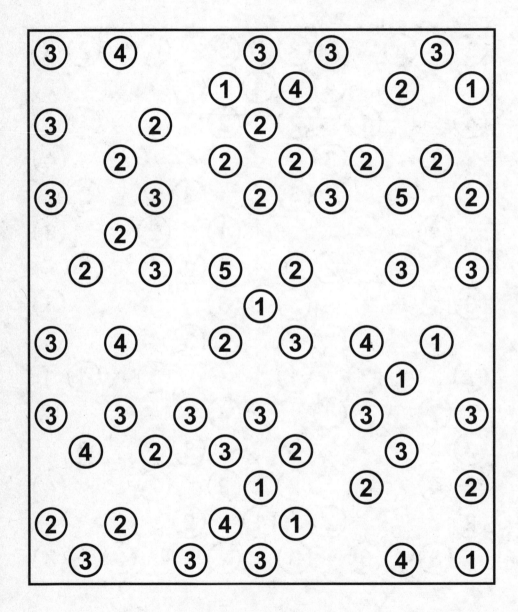

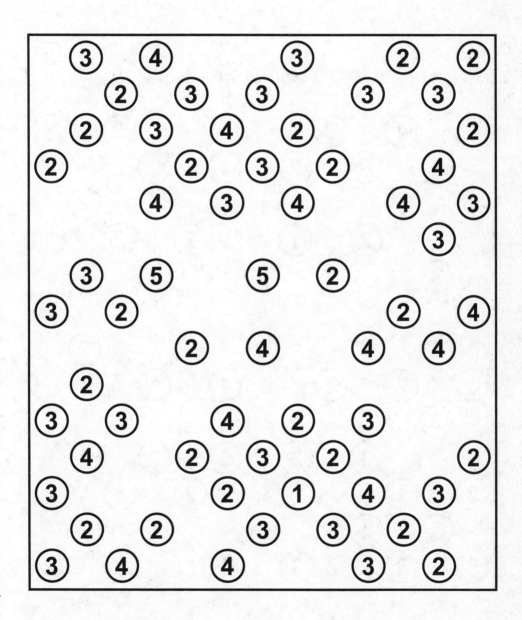

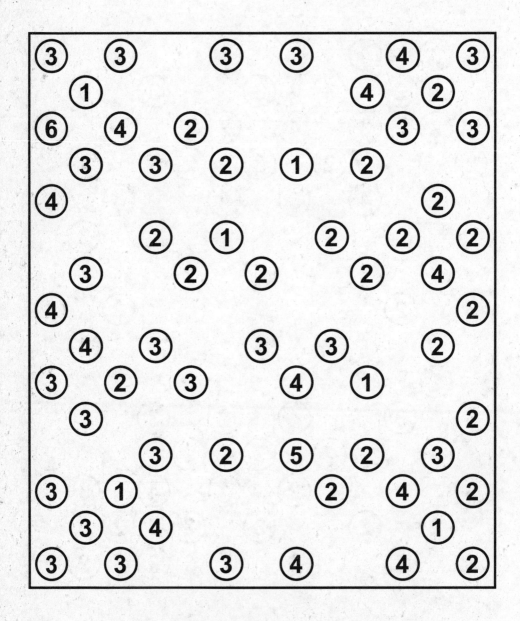

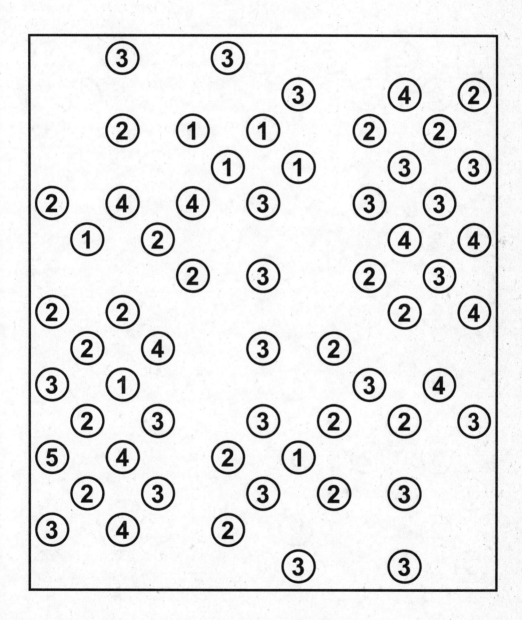

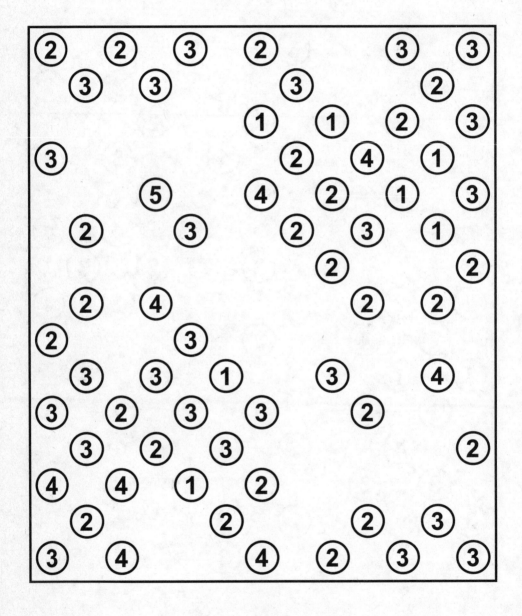

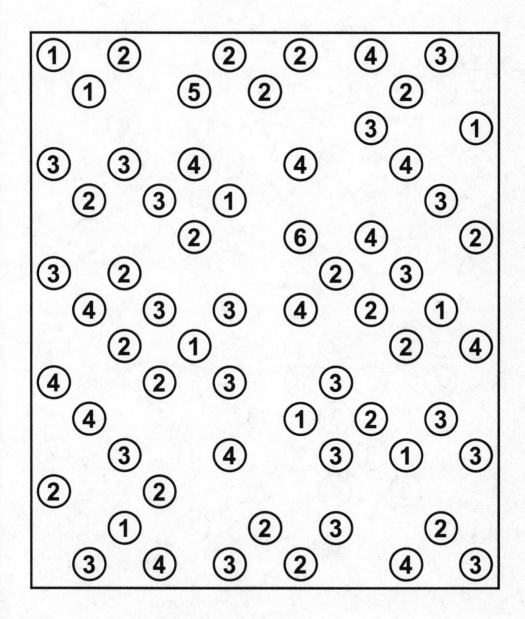

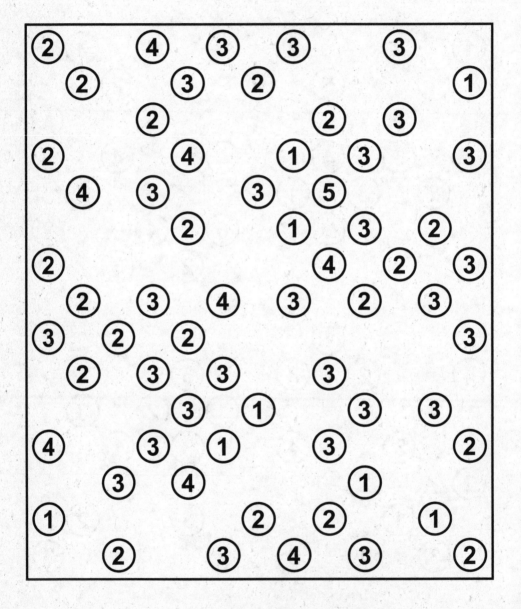

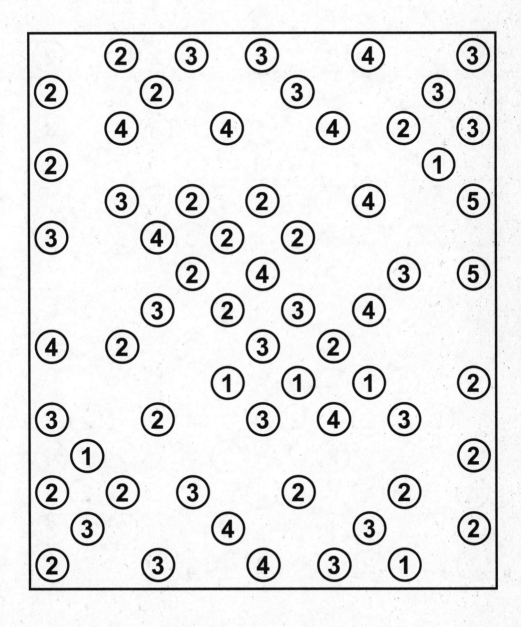

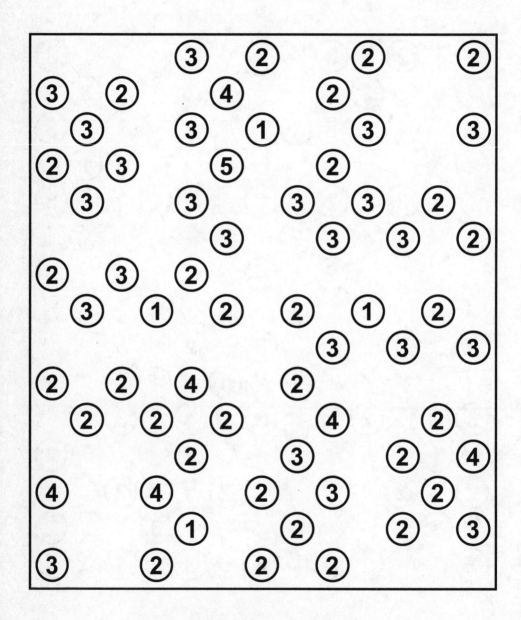

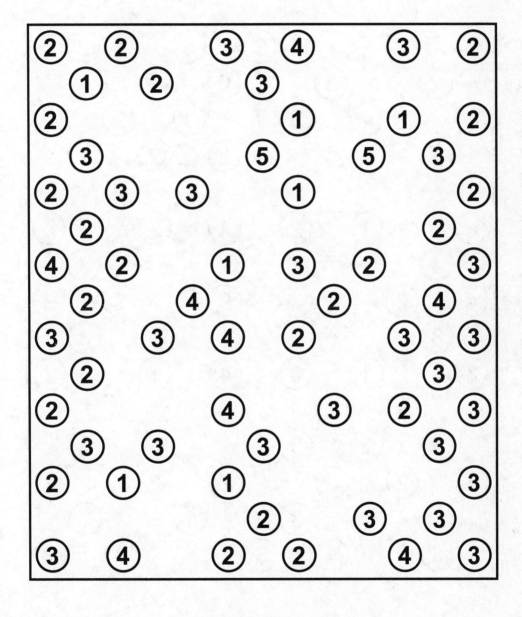

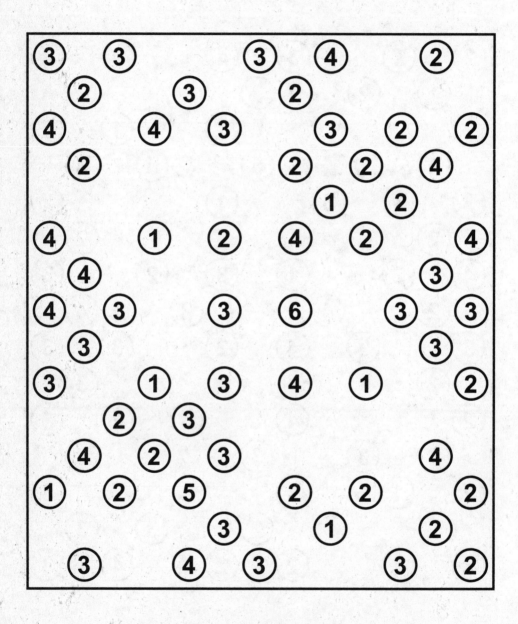

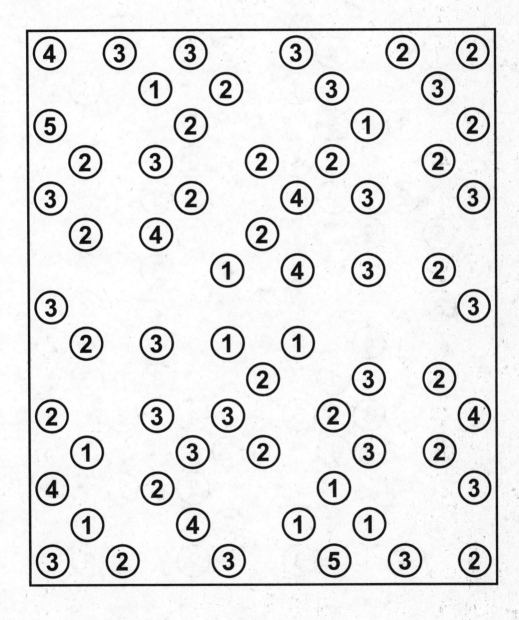

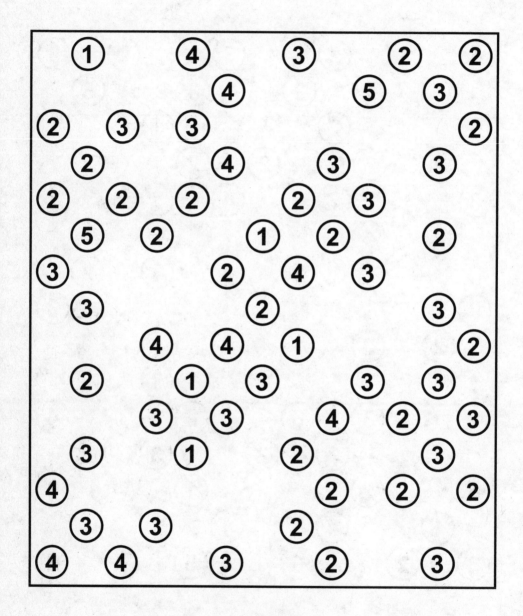

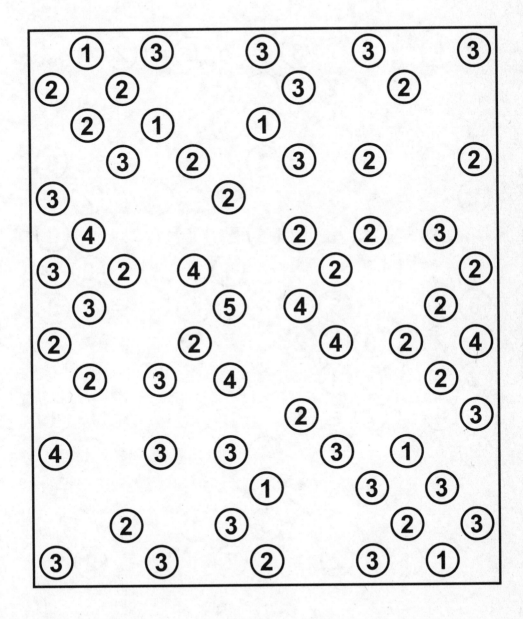

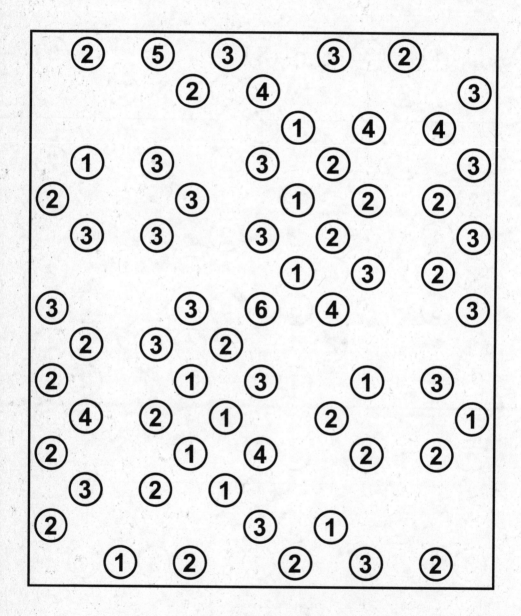

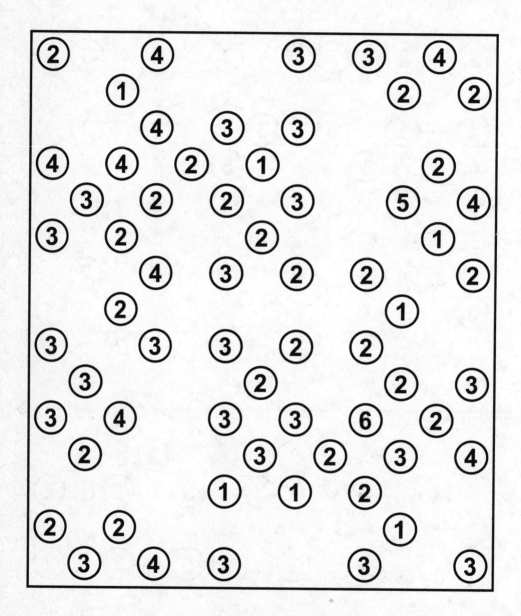

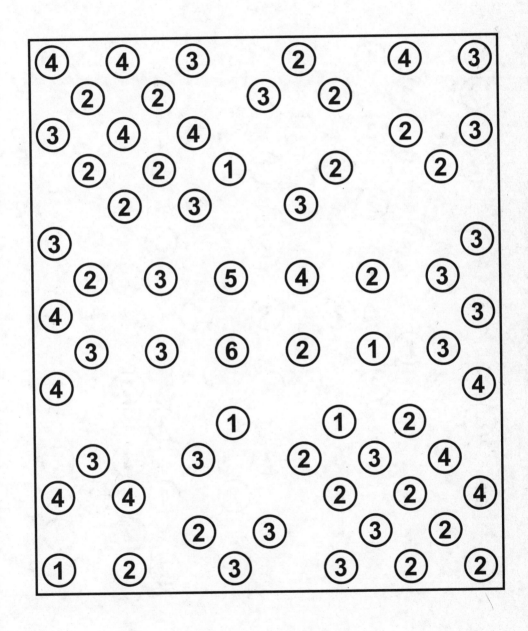

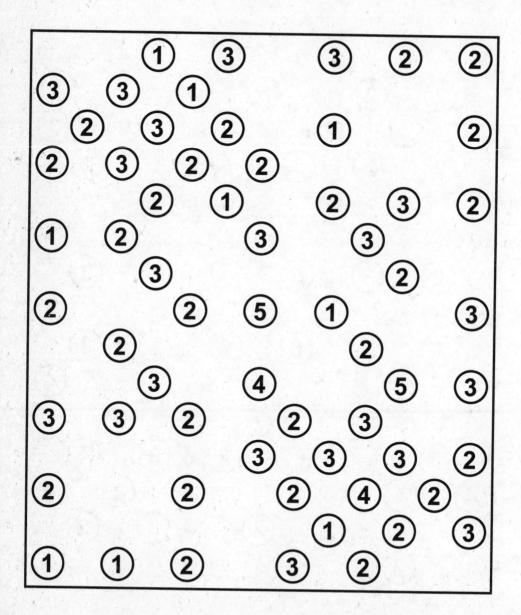

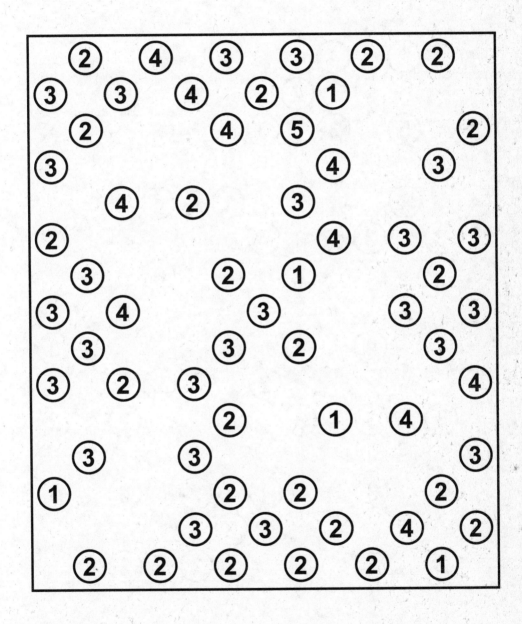

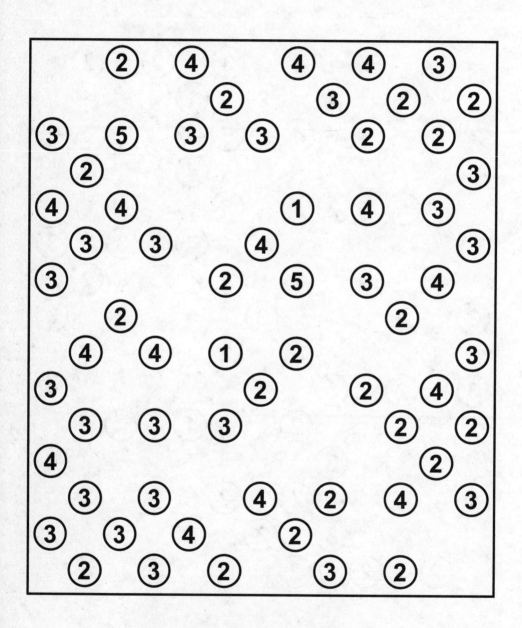

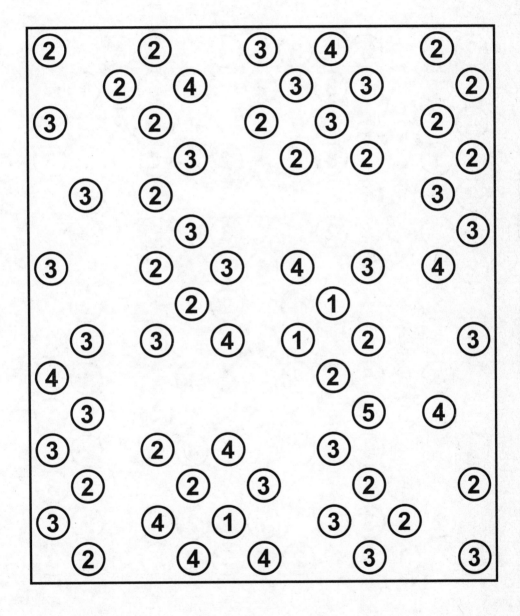

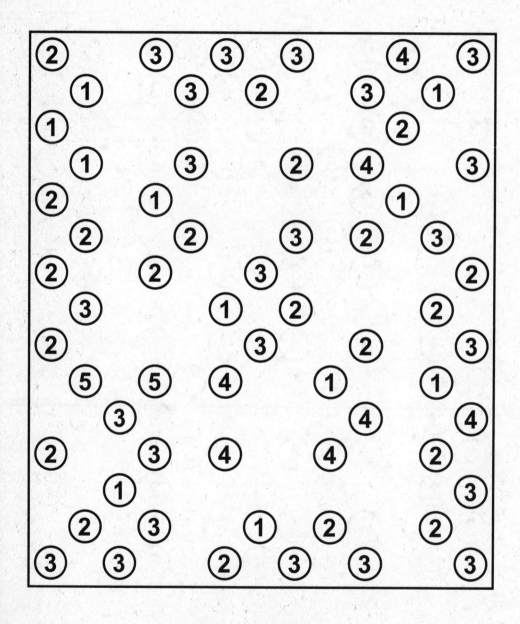

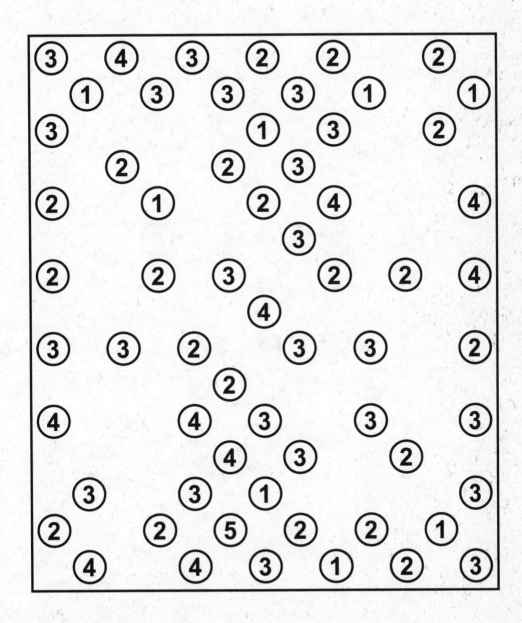

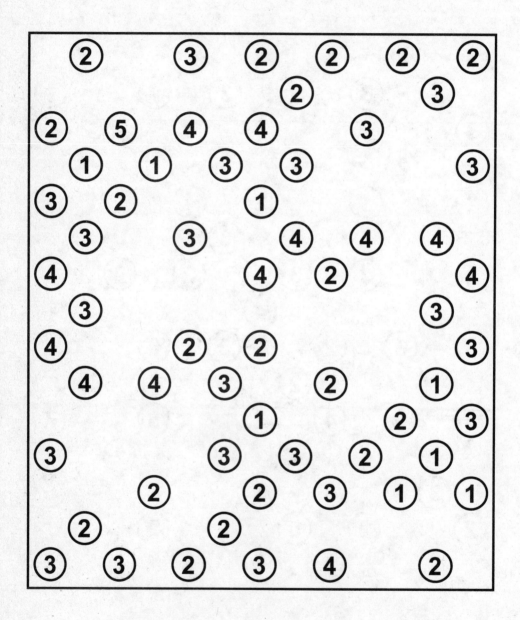

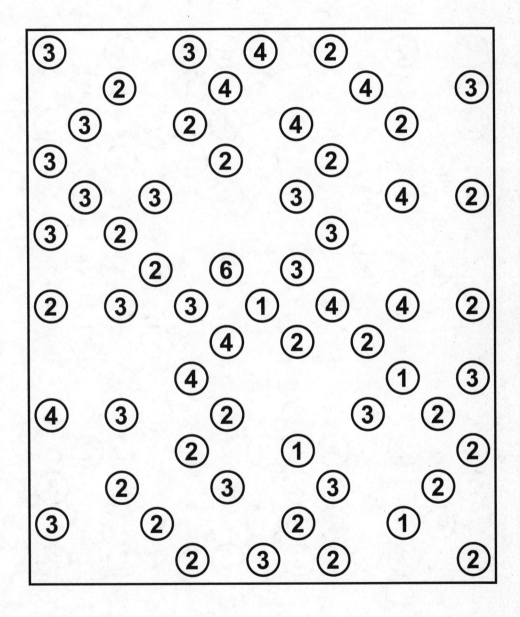

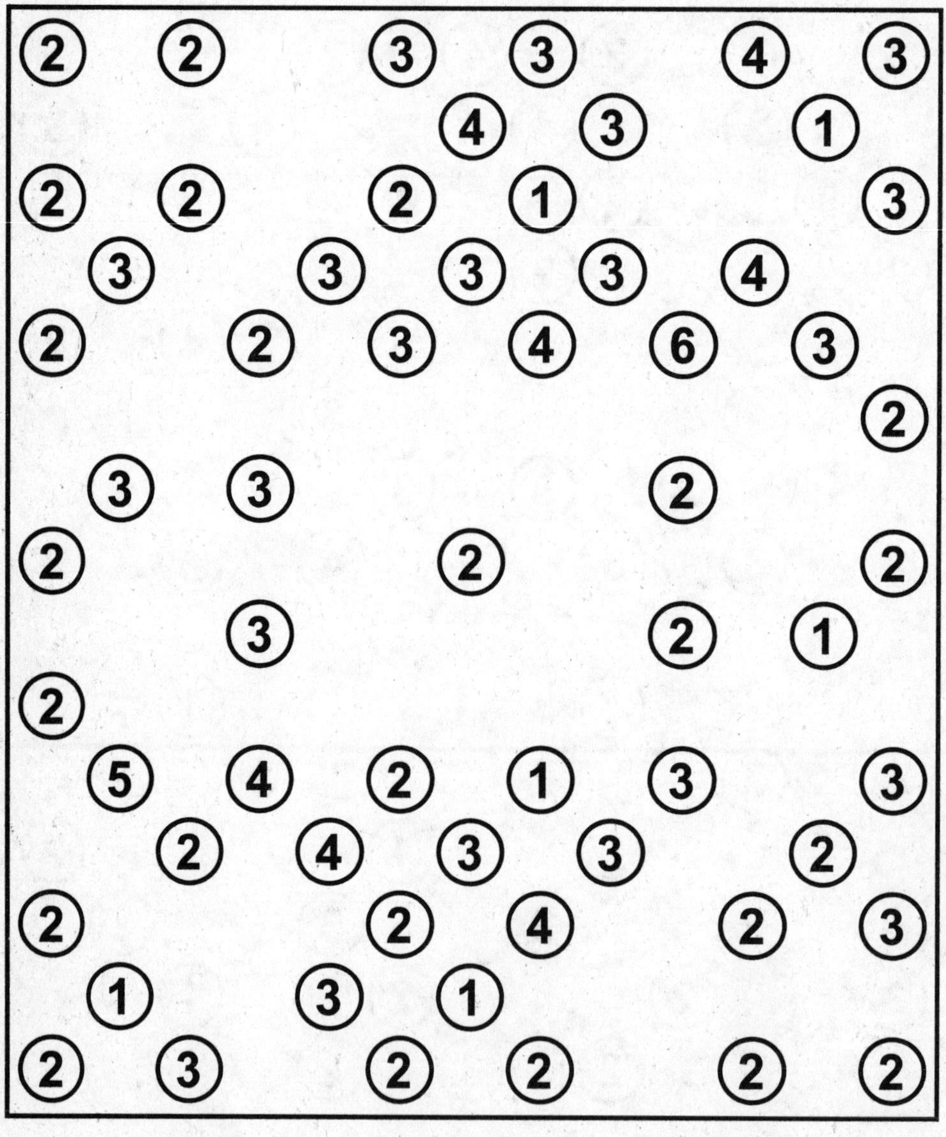

② ②　③ ③　④ ③
　　④ ③　①
② ②　② ①　③
③　③ ③ ③ ④
②　② ③ ④ ⑥ ③
　　　　②
③ ③　② 
② ②　②
③　② ①
②
⑤ ④ ② ① ③ ③
② ④ ③ ③ ②
② ② ④ ② ③
① ③ ①
② ③ ② ② ② ②

|SOLUTIONS|

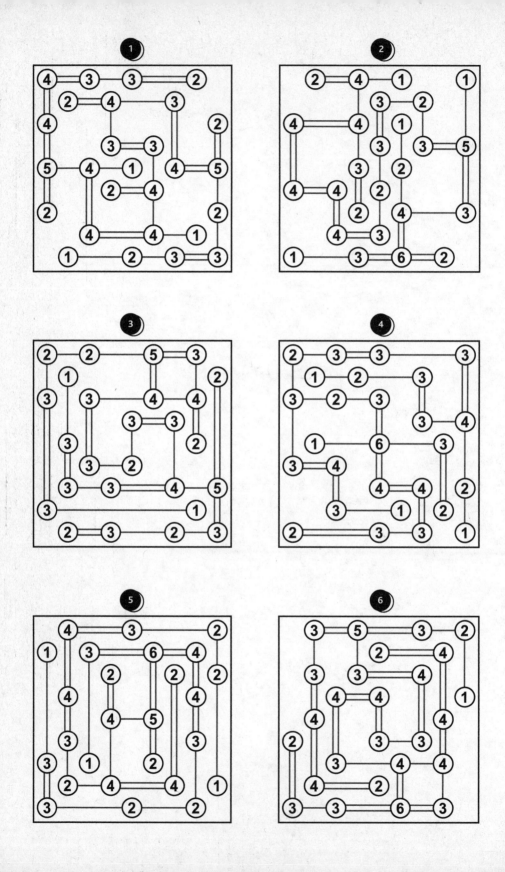

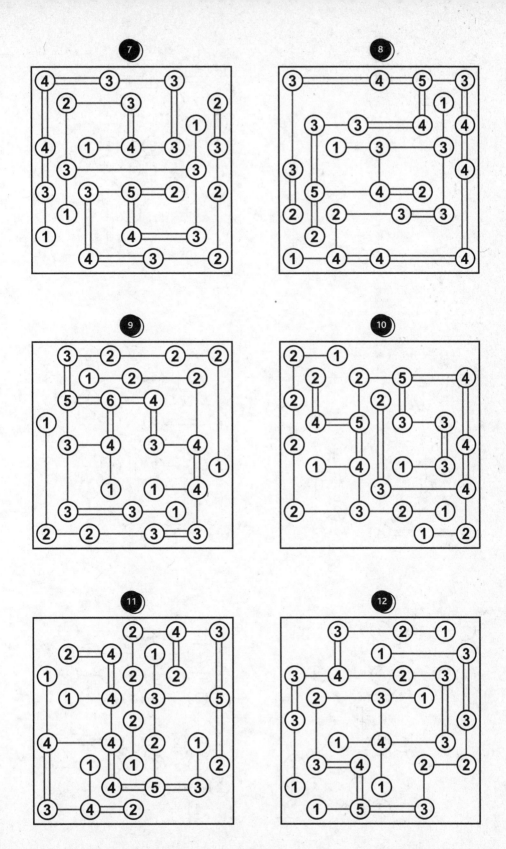

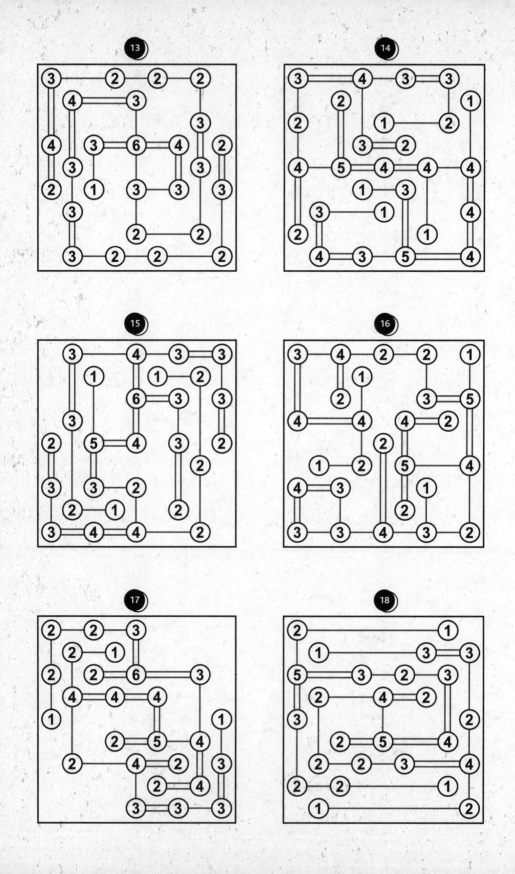

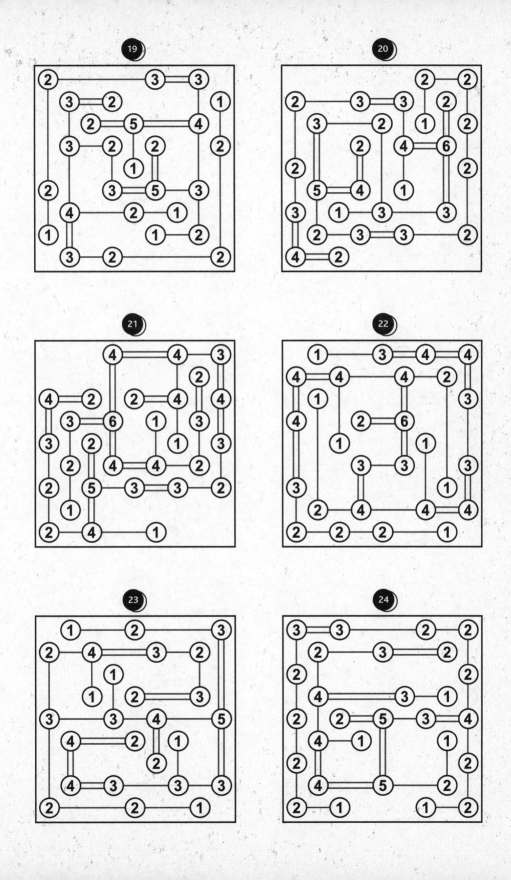

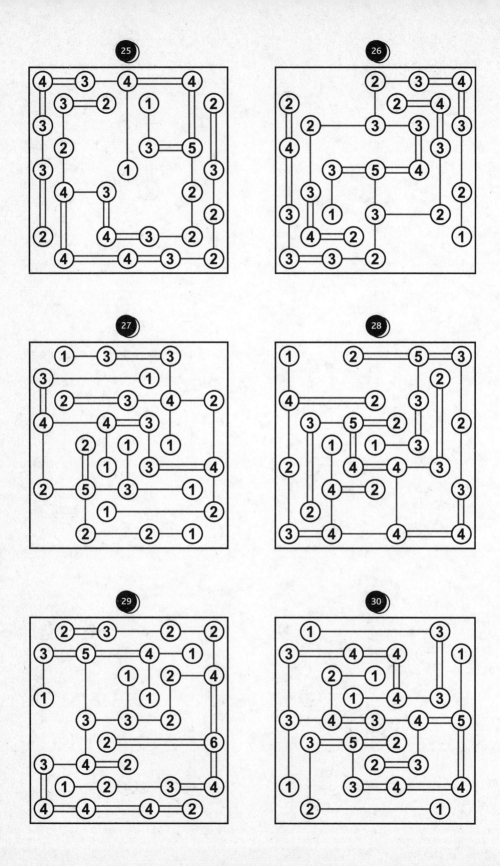

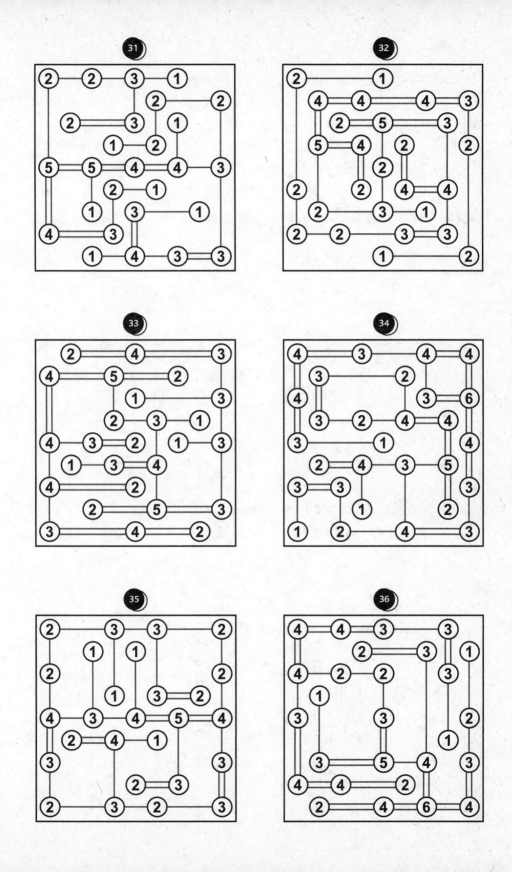

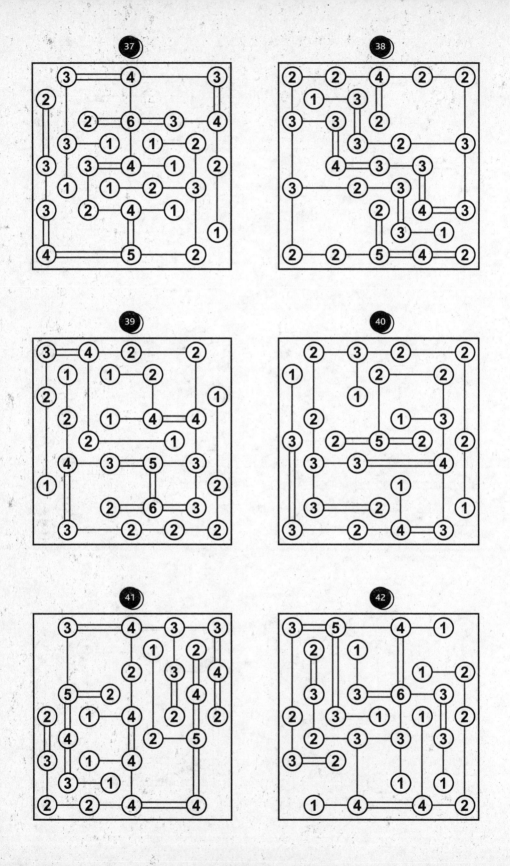

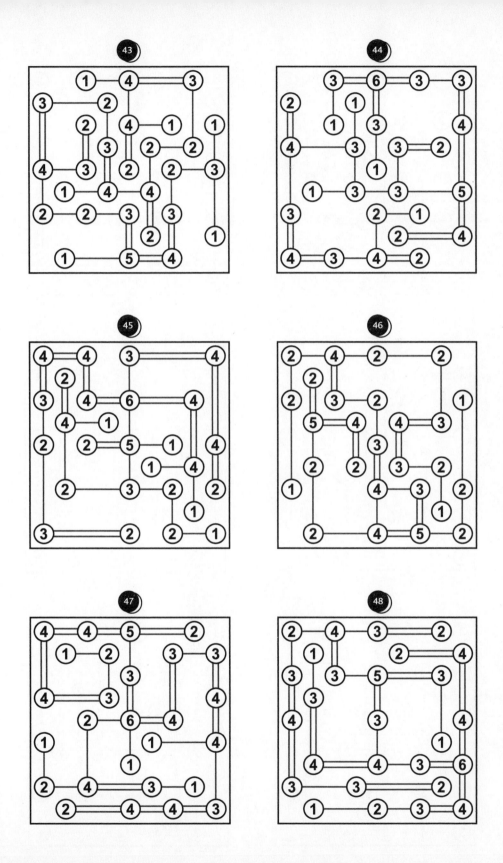

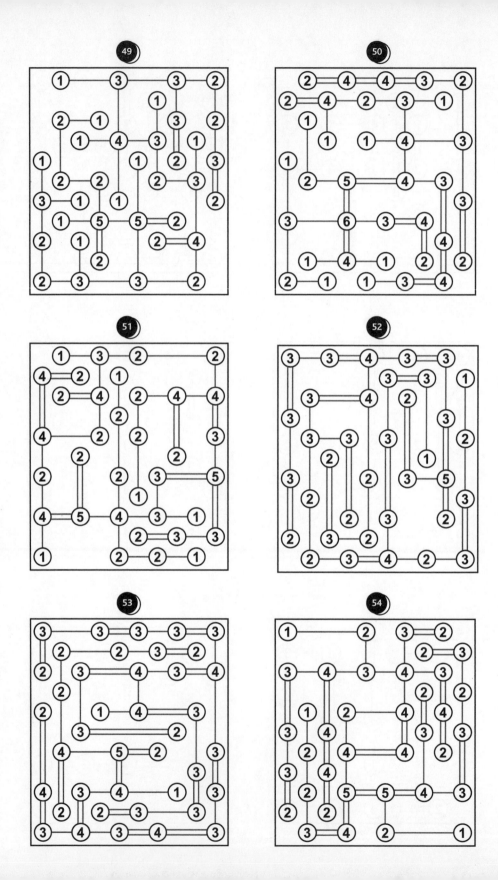

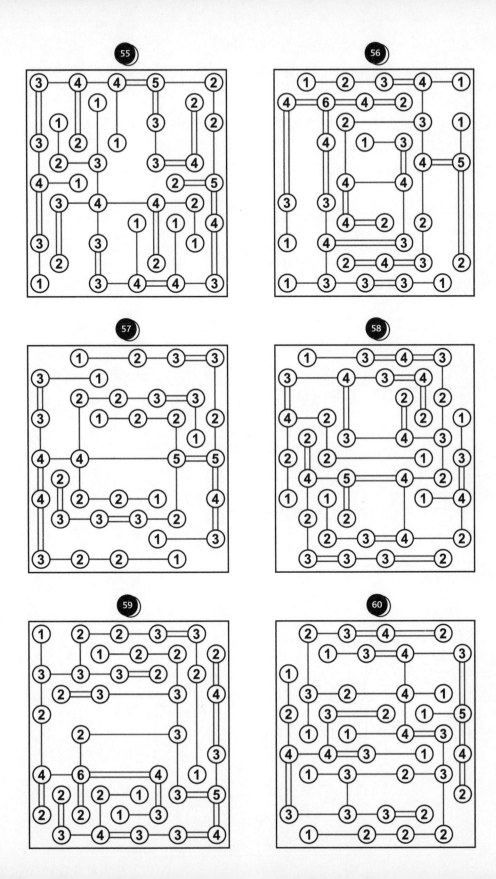

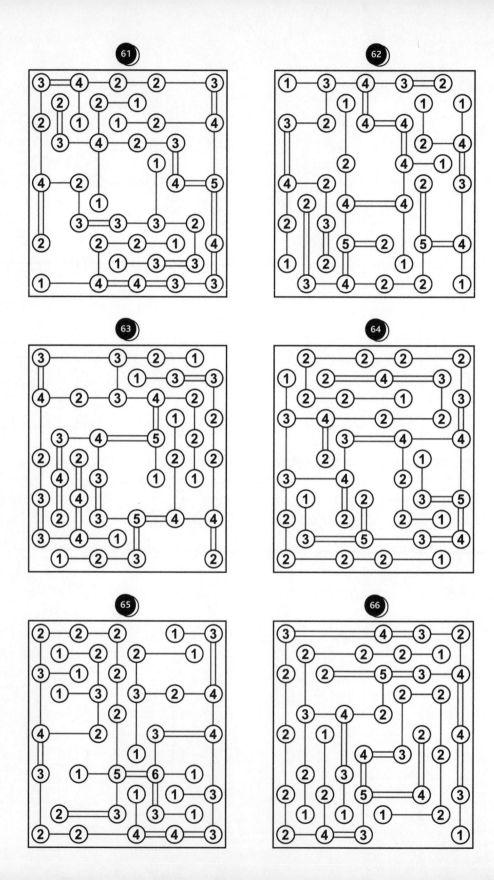

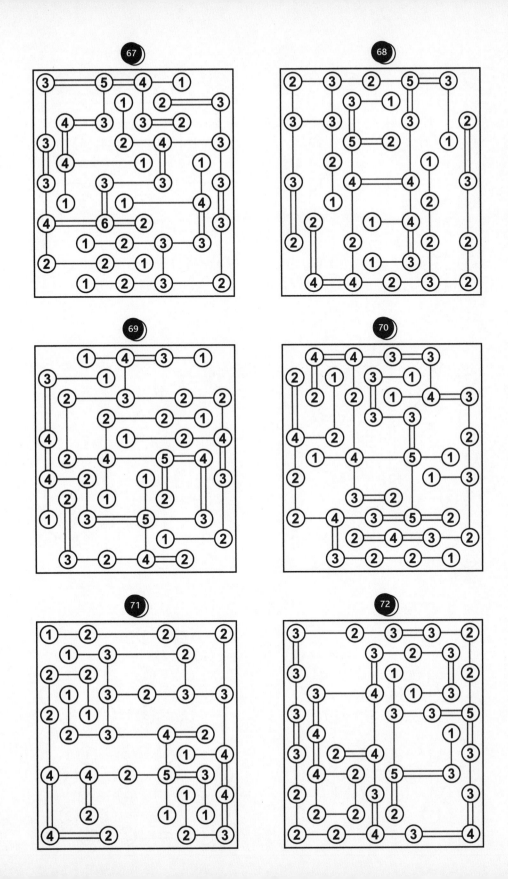

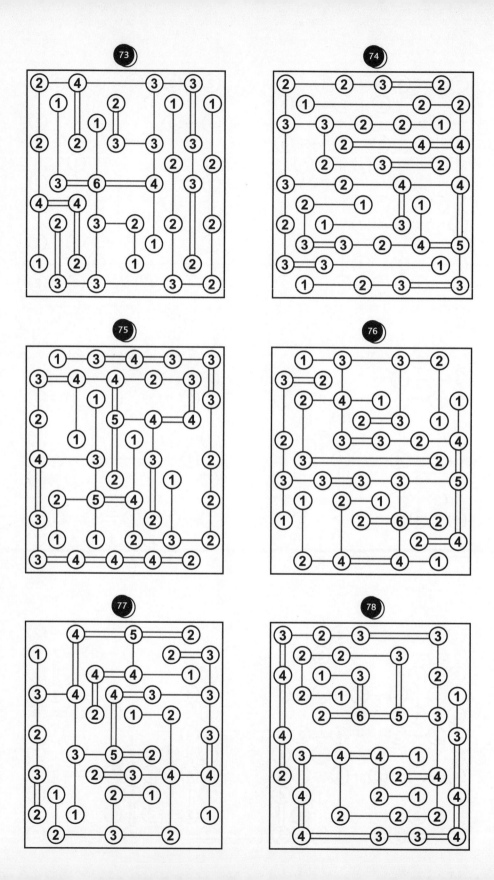

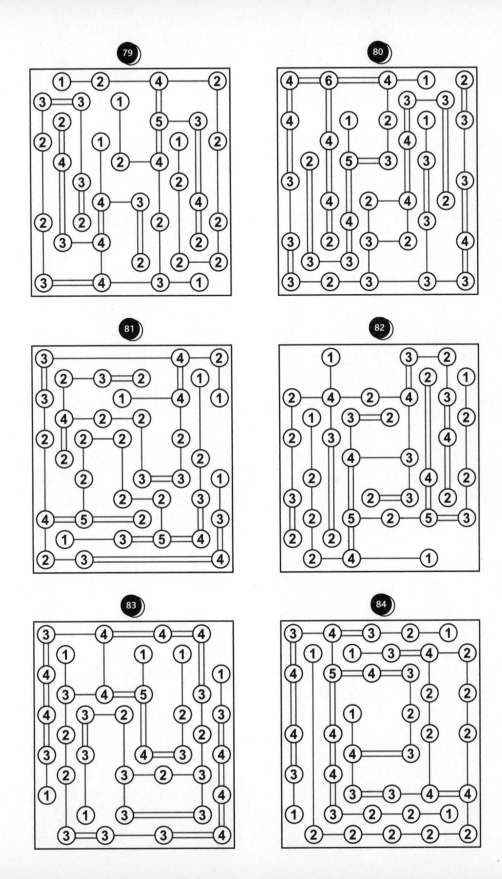

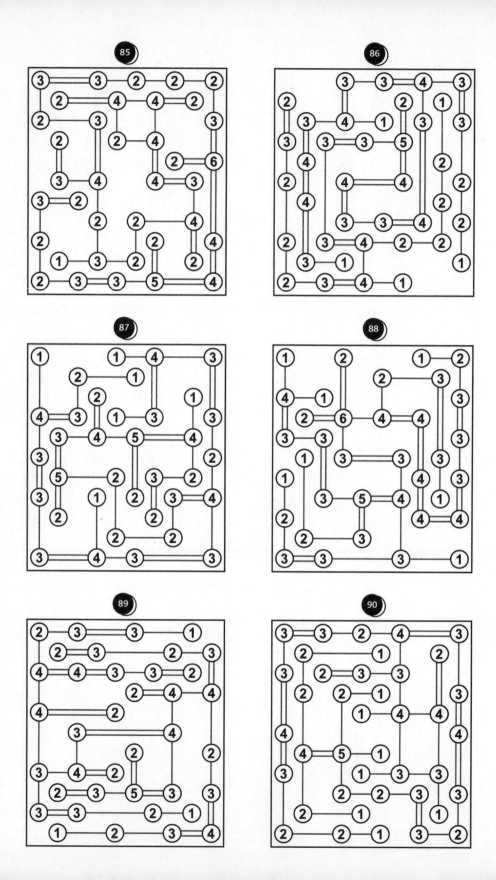

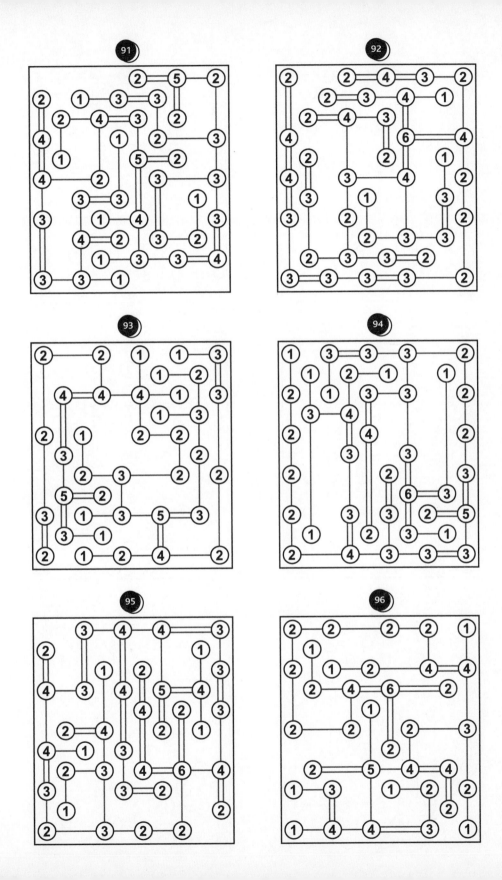

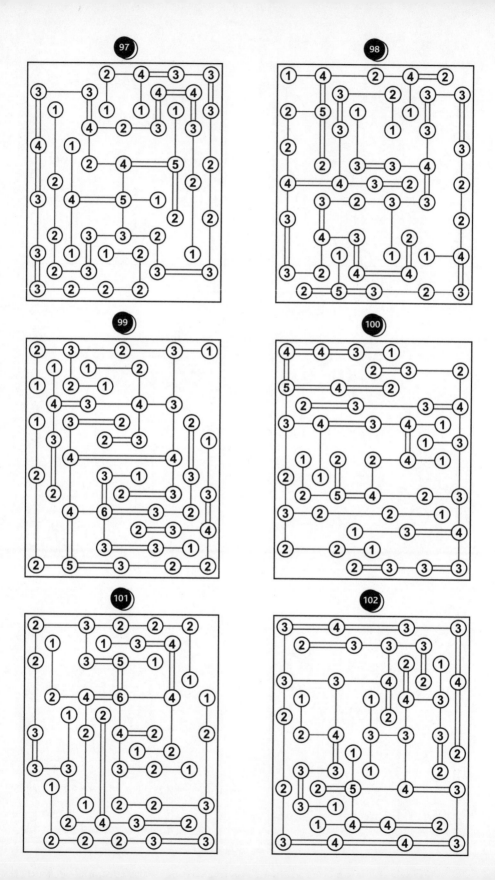

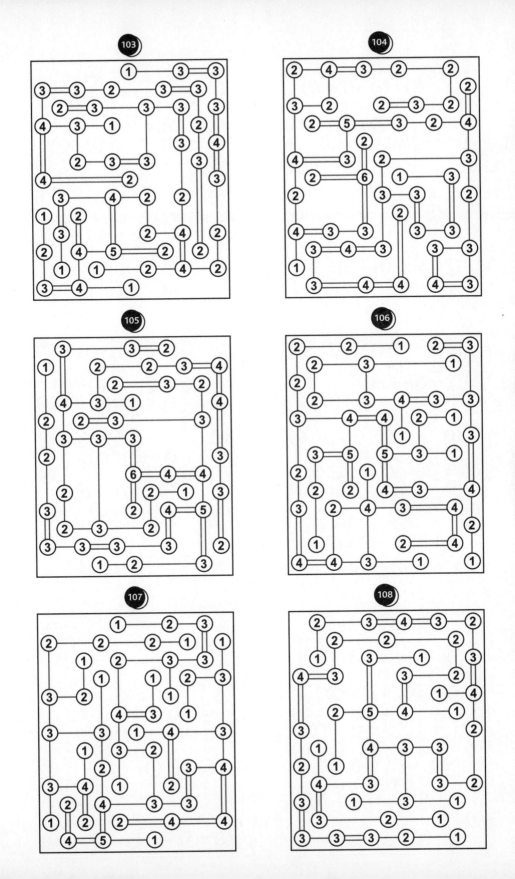

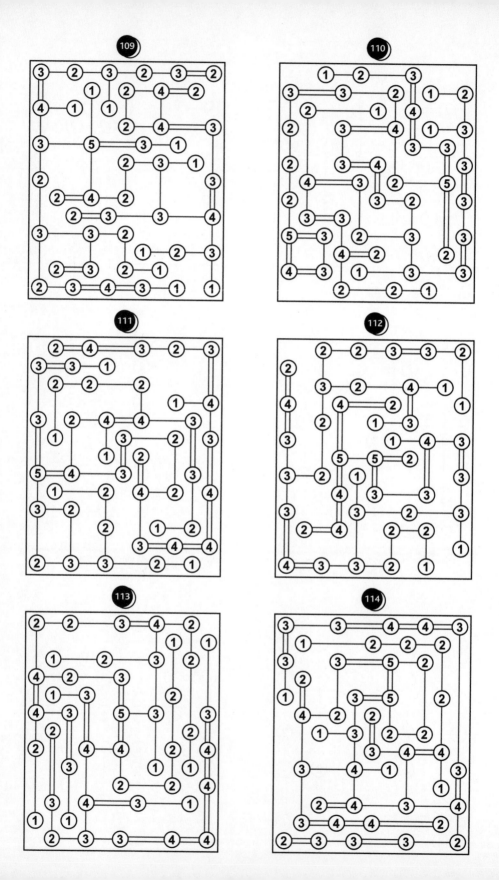

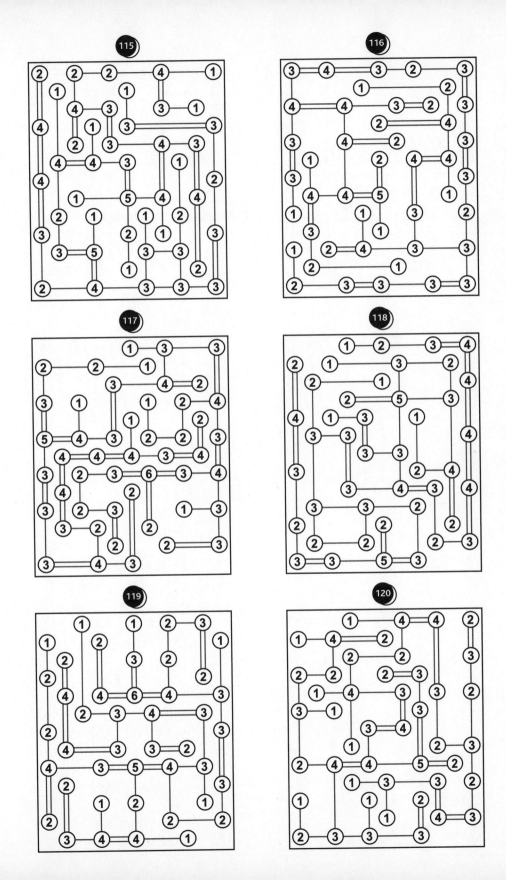

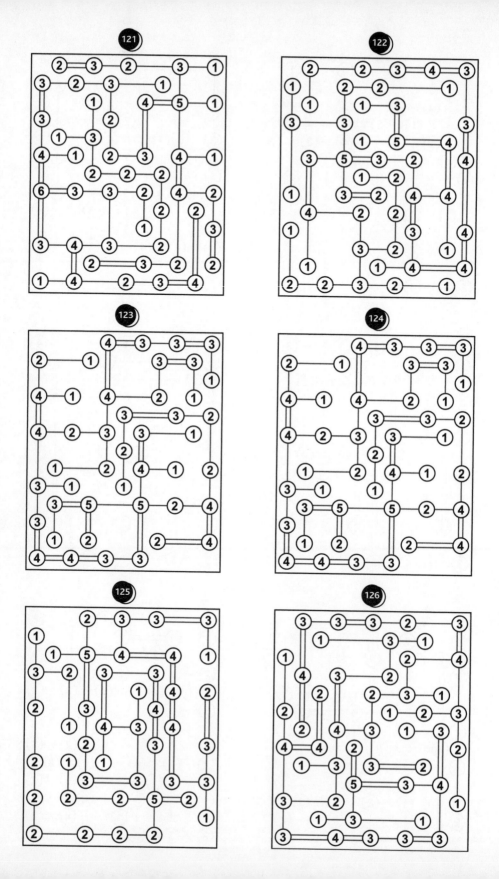

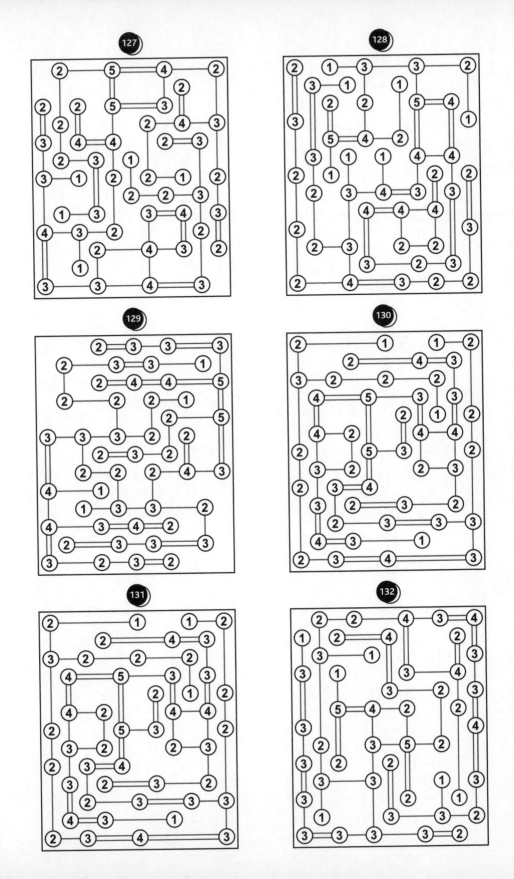

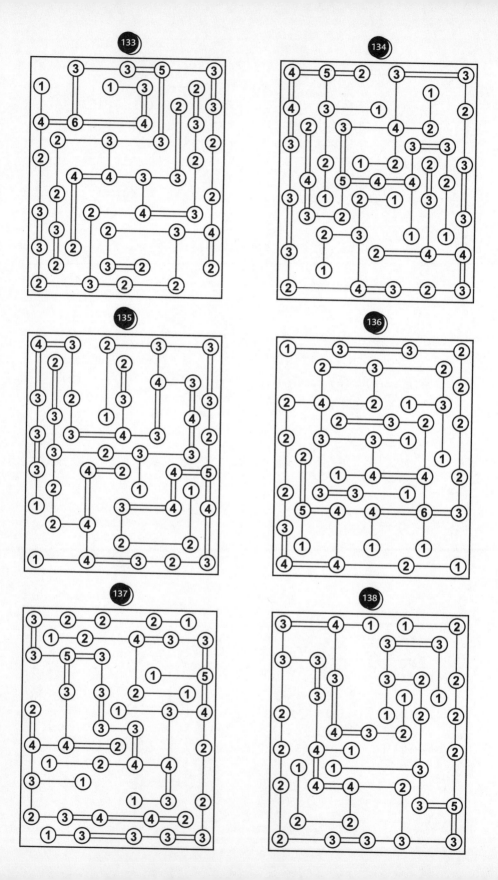

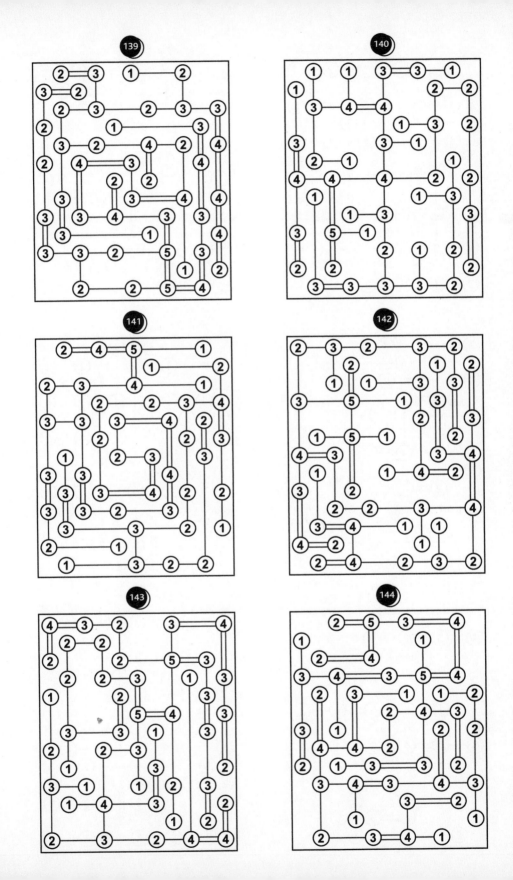

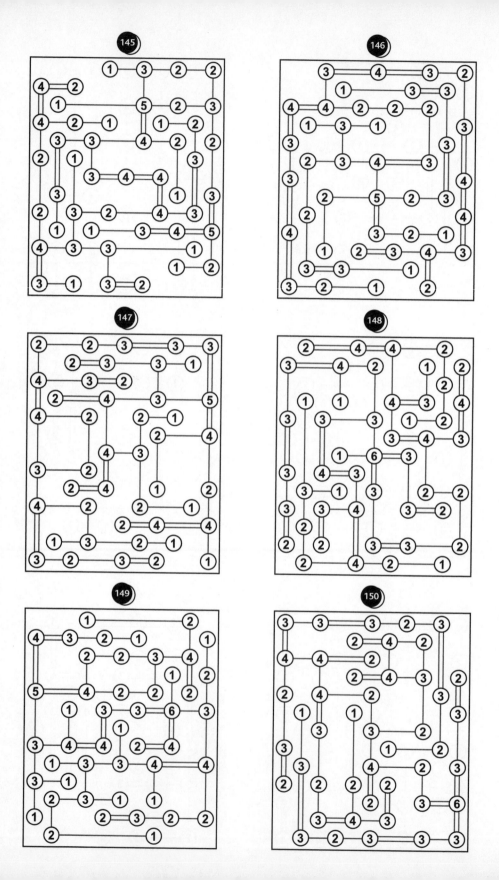

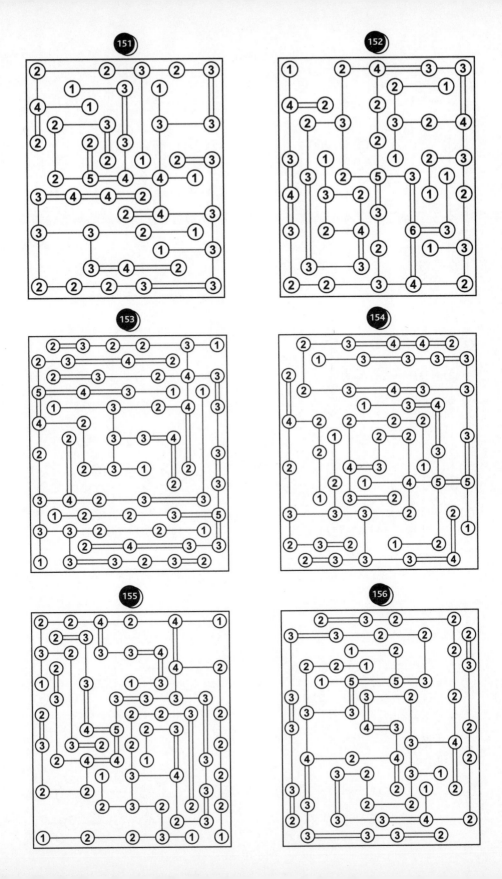

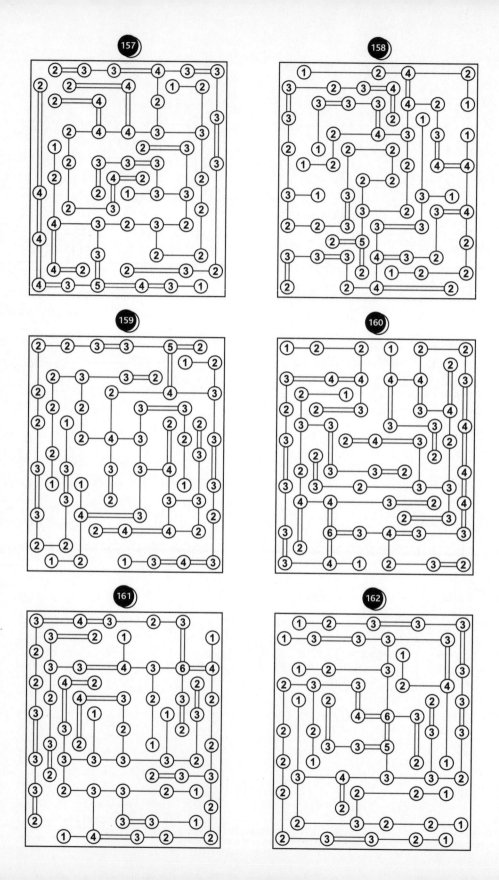

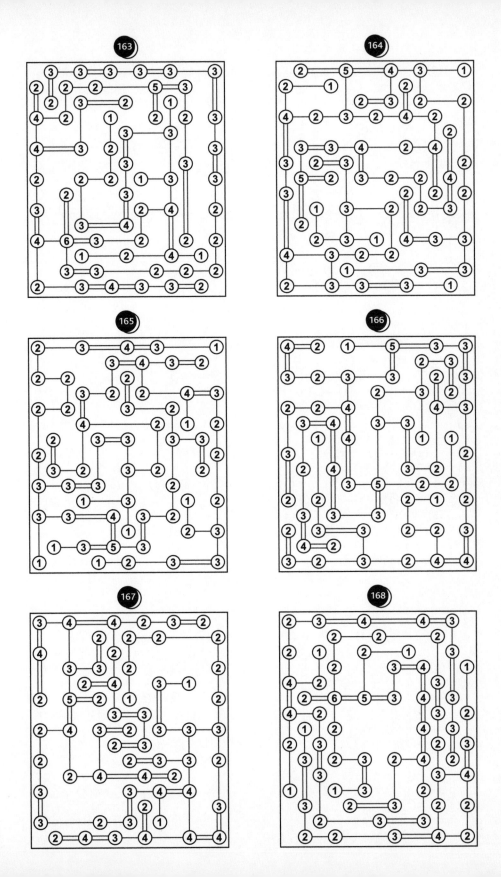

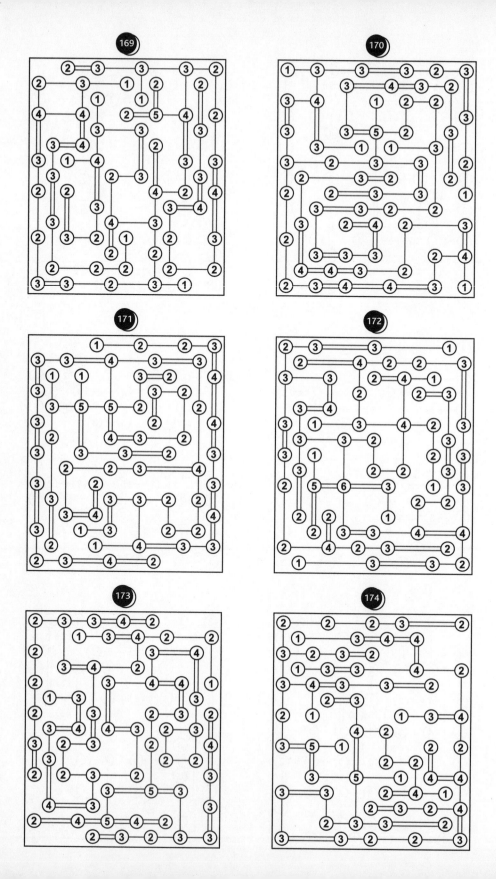

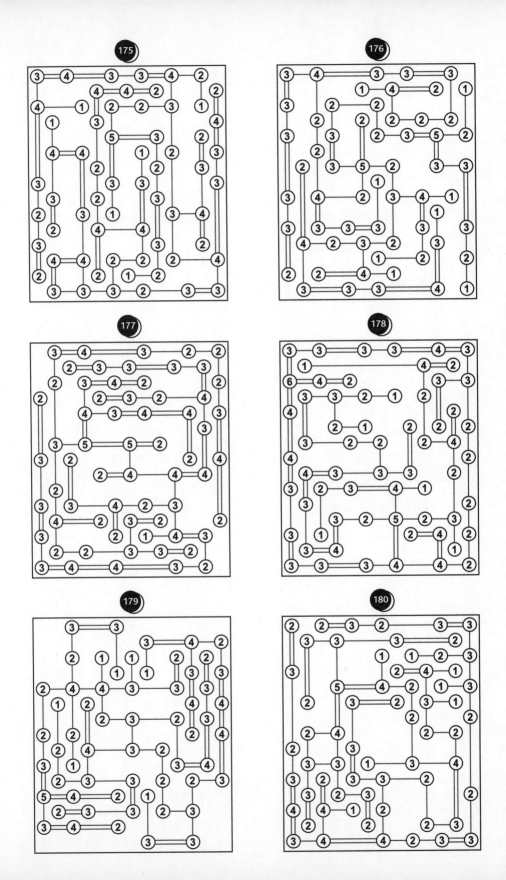

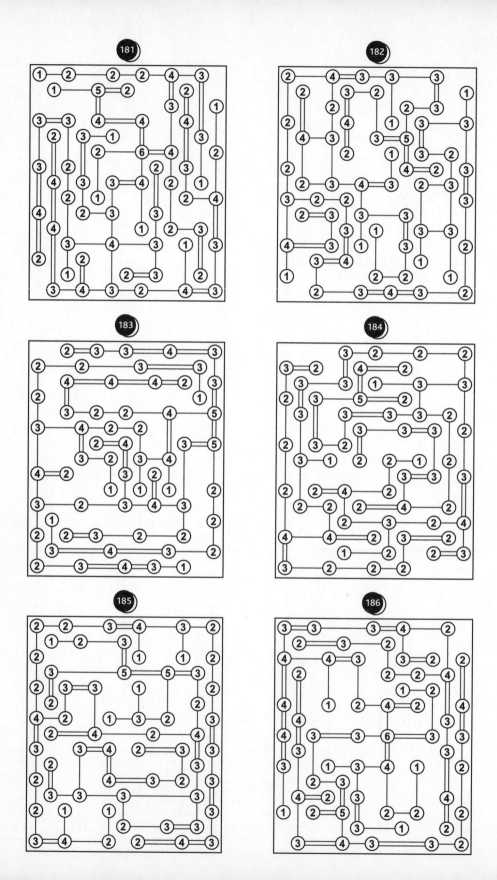

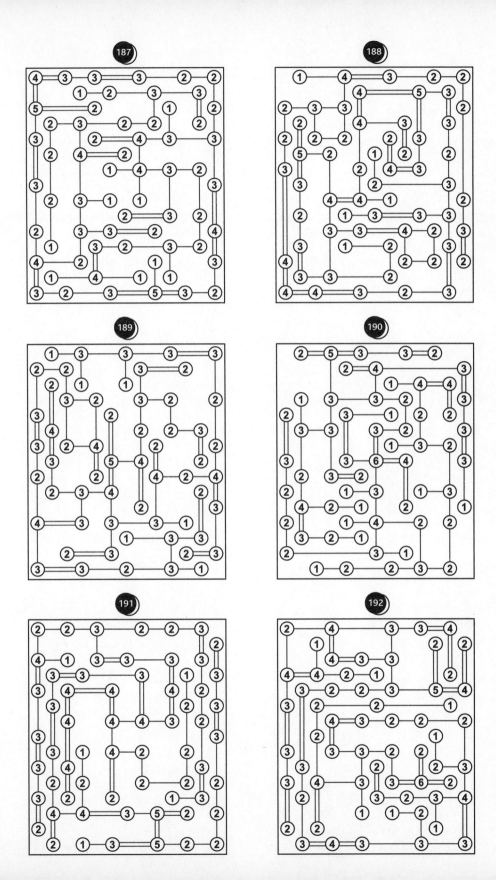

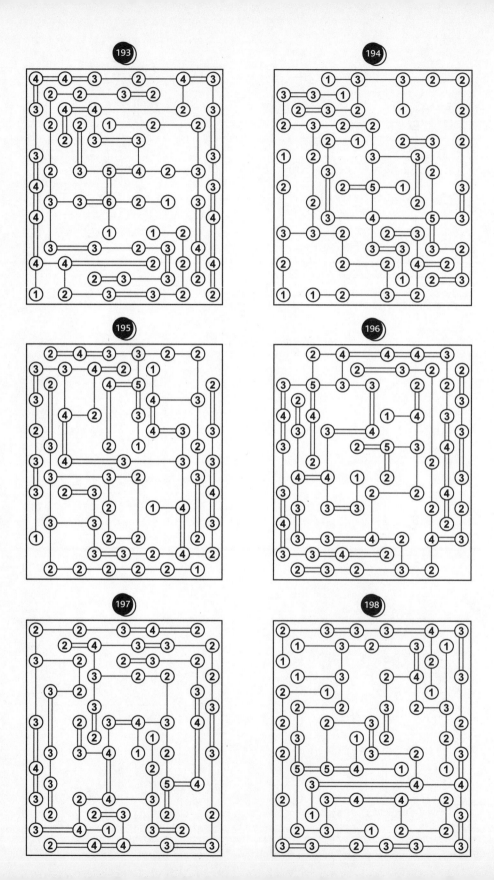

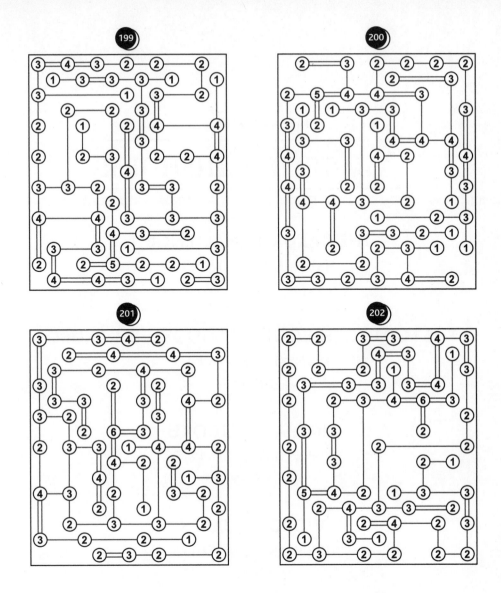

OTHER BOOKS BY

# ALASTAIR CHISHOLM

## THE KAKURO CHALLENGE 1

ISBN: 0-8027-1528-1

$8.95

## THE MAMMOTH BOOK OF SUDOKU & KAKURO

ISBN: 0-8027-1541-9

$8.95

## MONSTER SUDOKU

ISBN: 0-8027-1542-7

$8.95

## WORD SQUARES

ISBN: 0-8027-1561-3

$8.95

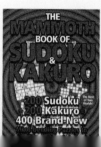
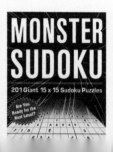

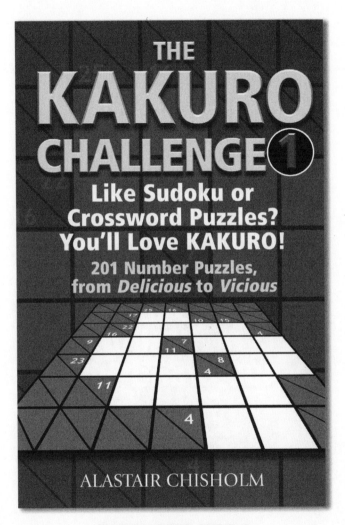

# THE KAKURO CHALLENGE 1

## Like Sudoku or Crossword Puzzles? You'll Love KAKURO!

### 201 Number Puzzles, from *Delicious* to *Vicious*

ALASTAIR CHISHOLM

ISBN 0-8027-1528-1
$8.95

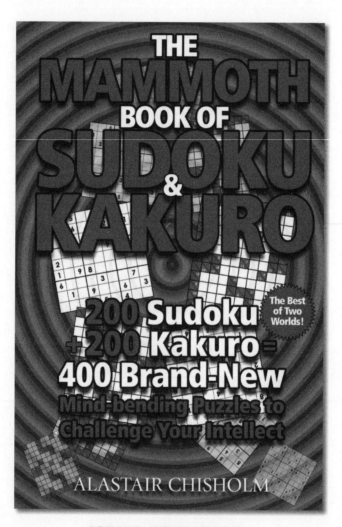

# THE MAMMOTH
## BOOK OF
# SUDOKU
# & KAKURO

## 200 Sudoku
## + 200 Kakuro =
## 400 Brand-New
### Mind-bending Puzzles to
### Challenge Your Intellect

**The Best of Two Worlds!**

ALASTAIR CHISHOLM

**ISBN 0-8027-1541-9**
**$8.95**

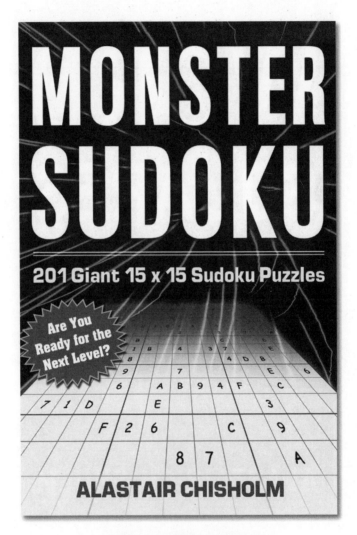

# MONSTER SUDOKU

## 201 Giant 15 x 15 Sudoku Puzzles

Are You Ready for the Next Level?

**ALASTAIR CHISHOLM**

ISBN 0-8027-1542-7

$8.95

# WORD SQUARES

## 201
FASCINATING WORD PUZZLES
FOR ANYONE WHO LOVES
CROSSWORDS OR
WORD JUMBLES

## ALASTAIR CHISHOLM

ISBN 0-8027-1561-3
$8.95